The story of William G. "Daddy" Weston—
a testimony of miracles and faith

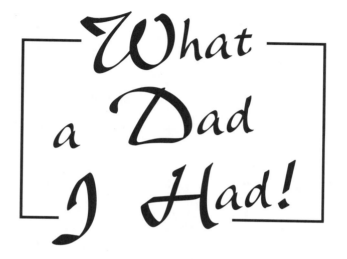

What a Dad I Had!

Bill Weston

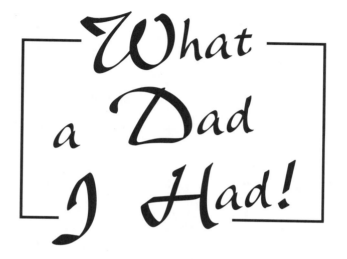

Christian Publications

CAMP HILL, PENNSYLVANIA

Christian Publications
3825 Hartzdale Drive, Camp Hill, PA 17011
www.cpi-horizon.com

Faithful, biblical publishing since 1883

ISBN: 0-87509-806-1

99   00   01   02   03   5   4   3   2   1

Unless otherwise indicated,
Scripture taken from the
Holy Bible: King James Version

CONTENTS

Bill, W. G.'s son, goes to reminiscing here in *What a Dad I Had!*

Did you ever try to write a book? First, just to find the time has been about as easy as putting a fresh oyster in a parking meter. Second, thoughts keep acrowding in, racing through my gray matter, and to even try and write all the things and times shared with Dad would keep a feller busier than a tattooed boat on the tummy of a seasick sailor.

Then, too, I simply HATE—and you all note I capitalized that word—to push a pen across paper, but since I can't type, the original manuscripts had to be jotted down via my inimitable scrawling, which created another chore, in that usually I can't decipher what I wrote in the first place. You see, I can read writing, but I can't write reading.

Where to begin was the first poser for me to un-snarl. I felt like the mosquito who, after lighting on a corpulent lady on the beach, knew what to do, but didn't know where to begin. For years I've been assembling all this material and now to sort it all out, unravel it, if you please, and get it to make sense to others on paper, by following a proper order, has driven me about as batty as a barefooted critter in the middle of an ant hill.

I'm traveling so much now in evangelism, like my dad did for so many years. May I revert to my terminology (just be me, right here) and say, "Boy! How I wish I could be even just half the man he was!"

Dr. Harold Freleigh, a truly great Bible scholar and teacher, and one of the sweetest saints that ever trod God's sod, one day in Canby Camp, Oregon, put his arms around me, hugged me close, and with tears in his eyes said, "Bill, I loved your father. We were dear friends. Well, Son, your dad's mantle has fallen on you. I know he's gone now, and we all miss him; but I want you to know this—it's a promise: I'll be your dad now and pray for you every day as he did."

Words like that will make a fellow gulp, swallow his Adam's apple and cause his eyes to puddle up and leak. If y'all could have known Dad Freleigh as I came to know him, then you would realize what those words did for yours truly. And pray for me he did until he too went home to be with the Lord he so dearly loved; and I lost another friend (another dad), but only for a little while.

Anyhow, during my travels—on planes, driving the highways, in a lonely motel room—my mind would occasionally come unraveled, would wander back across the years, and I'd just let her go. Because some of the happiest moments of my life are just remembering *What a Dad I Had!* So on the following pages, I share with you unforgettable memories, stories, tales and anecdotes that I'm certain will crinkle your face with a smile and fog up your eyes occasionally too. I will share from those early years, which are full of unforgettable sessions with Dad who, in spite of his busy schedule, always had time for his boy.

This book is dedicated to the memory of Dad, who in his very busy life and schedule, always had time for his kids—Bea, Bob and Bill—and that I know for sure. Also, to Mom, who with Dad was always there when we needed them. Believe it. We Weston young'uns were truly blessed in having such loving, God-fearing parents.

I know too, this book surely will not reach any best-seller list or be the best written as far as grammar, spelling, punctuation and other standards required by the really learned scholars and authors. No, not even by the wildest stretch of the imagination could that ever be said. Also, I'm certain, so-called intellectuals and writing critics will find a lot of flaws.

That reminds me of the real estate agent who, when selling a certain home, said to his prospective buyers, "Here's a house you will love. It hasn't any flaws." To which the startled down-home folks replied, "No flaws! Land sakes! Then what do y'all walk on?" I love stories like that.

I repeat, folks examining my skill in writing procedures will find my accomplishments in this area falling far short of what is usually acceptable to their intelligent way of thinking. But, you know what? It's the best book I could write and I'm plumb satisfied with what I've jotted down. Why? Because it accurately tells stories and events I recall that were to me some of the most precious times in my life. Besides, so many experts, as I have reason to believe, are more often than not a fellow with a briefcase away from home, or as one definition put it, "A drip under pressure," and that's a good one.

So, for any of such a bent, that can't recognize the pure artistry of my style in pushing a pen across paper, well (as former President Reagan would say), I couldn't be less concerned, for you see, several years ago I met someone who changed my way of thinking and writing.

While in Newton, Kansas for a city-wide evangelism crusade, I met a fellow who became a dear and beloved friend of mine. He told me, "Bill, listen boy, never change your way of putting down words on paper." I reckon he must have read one of my inimitable letters to one of my friends—those who have received same, will know what I'm a saying here. Anyhow, that man was a very special person to me. And he just happened to be the former speech writer for Franklin Delano Roosevelt, President of the USA, and daily wrote a column that appeared on the very front page of a statewide newspaper called The Kansan. His work appeared under the title "Fiddlin' with Fagan."

Mr. Fagan's articles were read by all and sundry with many a chuckle and grin creasing the weather-beaten "fizzogs"—that's "faces" to the un-larned in down-home language—of those Kansas farmers, as he described the doings of the day. And, I must add here, there was nary a sign of criticism of this famed writer nor his style of penmanship. Talking to the local citizenry I found he was one of the best loved men in that part of our country. Words like the following appeared daily in his beloved column in the newspaper: cuz, sez, tis, ain't and larnin'. You see, it was all down-home talk to folks out thataway—as he put it, "folks who haint larned yet how to be snooty." Enough said.

So I'm certain I have my friend's endorsement for what's written on the following pages if ya'll care to peruse same.

CHAPTER ONE

Earliest Memories

This story begins with this writer's entrance into this world on June 29, 1914 in Trafford City, PA—William Todd Weston, son of W. G. and Tessie Woodring Weston. The first few years I can't remember, but there was a lot of tender loving care provided by Mom, Dad and my ten-year-old sister, Bea.

Things began to really come into focus for me when as a wee lad I used to dig a hole under a backyard fence (constructed to keep this young pup in) so I could scurry across two sets of streetcar tracks and a big open field to get to my Pop at the Lesher Lumber Yard.

Then, too, I faintly recall a soldier suit, so I could look like my daddy who like millions of others was involved in World War One. I so vividly recall the rag and straw effigy of the Kaiser hanged and then burned on a gallows as America celebrated the cessation of the gory conflict and my Dad came marching home.

Another incident that is indelibly imprinted in the memory section of my mind was a very traumatic experience. I disobeyed my parents' instructions, ran into the street and was knocked down by a Model-T Ford. I scared the driver, Harry Gethin, nigh out of his drawers. Closing my eyes I can still see those four spoked wheels astride of me. Then I recall scooting out the back end and running like a scared ape because I figgered my pa and ma would sure dust off my western hemisphere for such a stupid act of disobedience.

At the time, Dad was shaving in our upstairs bathroom. When he heard Harry's bulb horn and the squeal of tires, he looked out and saw the whole thing. He first contemplated jumping out of that second story window, but thought better of it. He came tearing down the stairs and out and up the street after me. You could say he was in a real lather when he caught up to me. But, you know, instead of initiating the back of my front, he grabbed me up in his arms and hugged and hugged me. "Oh, thank the Lord!" he kept saying, "Thank the Lord!" At my tender age I didn't rightly know what the Lord had to do with it, but I was all for the apparent results.

Later, at eight years of age, I had a second encounter with a moving vehicle. It happened while one of my school chums and I were playing tag. In the excitement, he pushed me too hard and I landed right in the path of a big Mack truck. I really experienced a run down feeling as I mighty near didn't survive that accident. I was out of school for six weeks and will bear the scars of that occasion the rest of my daze—I got hit in the head. Reckon that explains a lot of things about yours truly to many of my friends. Tsk!

Many years later, in North Miami Beach, Florida, I saw Harry Gethin. He was in his nineties by then and when I rapped on the screen door, I saw someone quick—well, as quick as a 91-year-old can with two speeds, slow and stop—sneak out of the room and across the hallway. Bless his old heart, he was wearing those old-fashioned long johns, you know, the drop-leaf-table type. Anyhow, he grabbed a bathrobe, which his wife thought made him much more presentable, and came to the door. As we talked, he still remembered vividly that day in 1919 when I ran out in front of his old Model-T. Shucks, come to think of it, it really couldn't have hurt me much. Engines only had about 25 mouse power back then, I reckon.

While I was still a youngster, my family made a move from Trafford City, PA to Elizabeth, PA—a little town nestling in the hills on the banks of the Monongahela River, just about eleven miles upstream from the city of McKeesport, PA. In later years, I used to call it a poke and plumb town. You say, "What's that?" Well, that's a town that's so small if you poke your nose around the corner, you're plumb out of town. In fact, it was so small the signs for city limits were back to back. But there was one thing in its favor—we didn't have any crime in our streets. Well, we had crime, but no streets. Anyhow, it was and still is home to me and mine. It's always great to return to old scenes where memories go swirling through your mind as you recall so many events.

It was here I began my schooling under the tutelage of one of the sweetest people I've ever met—a real lady, my first-grade teacher, Miss Hannah Stevens. She learned me so much, and like so many tykes, I fell in love with my first grade teacher. She could do no wrong. She never did marry although I'm certain any number of us boys in her class would have "altared" that situation if only she'd have quit adding on years and waited for us.

I didn't like the term "old maid." Nope! Miss Stevens, as we respectfully called her, was, as I figured, just a monument to some man's stupidity. We never did know her age. She would smile when asked and just sort of clam up or switch the subject. You see, even back then, gals fibbed about their age. Reckon that's always been a female trait, because I'm certain even back in the Stone Age when they wrote down such data they were probably chiseling. Tsk!

Here's a wee poem I heard once that fits in here.

> Here lies the bones of Susan Jones.
> For her, life held no terrors.
> She lived an old maid.
> She died an old maid.
> No hits. No runs. No errors.

In those early formative years, Dad was an integral part of my life, even in my schooling. He and our principal were friends. They wrote notes to each other on occasion, and guess who delivered them? Anyhow, when I'd had any difficulty at school I could also expect a chain reaction at home. Dad taught me astronomy. When I'd see him take off his coat, roll his sleeves up, I knew that night there'd be spots on the son and the son wouldn't feel like setting. Yep, rolled up sleeves indicated we were going on a "wailing" expedition. I was to assume the position—head towards the North Pole, feet towards the South Pole—and then, he'd work on my equator. Wow! Did the temperature ever rise in that zone!

With my dad, "No" meant just that—"No!" To my dismay, he'd never read any of those modern

books on psychology about how you mustn't pun-
ish the little darlings because you might blight their
precious personalities. Man, he blighted mine!

With our move to Elizabeth, PA, my father became the manager and part owner of the West Elizabeth Lumber and Supply Company. What
tremendous business acumen he possessed! Within
just a few short years that company was shipping
truckloads of building material and lumber into a
tristate area.

The reason God so marvelously prospered this
man who loved his Lord and Savior Jesus Christ is
simple. He honored his heavenly Father with his
substance. His tithes and offerings came off the top
and into God's coffers first before household pay-
ments were made. Truly, the man who honors God,
God will honor.

The Father's wish for all His children is found in
Third John 2: "Beloved, I wish above all things that
thou mayest prosper and be in health, even as thy
soul prospereth." Dad believed that promise was
for real, like all the rest of the precious promises
contained in His Book. And his faith was tested on
more than one occasion.

One day three multimillionaire businessmen
from Pittsburgh came to my father's office in
West Elizabeth. You've met the type—selfmade
men. If you are ever privileged to meet one of
these characters (and believe me, they are characters) take a good gander at them, because there's
a prized example of unskilled labor. Anyhow, to
continue, their compliments on the success of his
company seemed genuine. Along with a lot of
other things, they told Dad, "Weston, it's noth-

ing short of amazing what you've done with this concern here!"

The upshot of it all was that these wealthy men were planning a syndicated program that would eventually squeeze out the little dealer and eventually control the lumber interests for the whole area. They wanted Dad to come in with them in this venture, but the more they talked, the less he liked the smell of things.

Finally Dad spoke. "Gentlemen," he said, "I deeply appreciate your generous praise and the fact that you want me to participate in your plans, but I don't think my partner would go along with such a contractual agreement. You see, it's this way. I've had it in my heart and I'm certain my partner concurs, that we want to help other lumber dealers, not force them out of business. This company here was once very small and struggling, but with my partner's wisdom and help it's become what you see today. I really can't take any credit because, you see, my partner contributed the lion's share in this operation and its success is totally due to his oversight."

Those Pittsburgh millionaires reacted as you'd naturally expect. "Who is he?" they wanted to know. "How come we never met him or heard his name mentioned? We've researched you thoroughly, Weston, and we didn't even know you had a partner. Let us talk to him. Where could we reach him?"

Dad smiled and said, "Gentlemen, He's here and yet He isn't here."

One broke in with, "What kind of double talk is that—he's here and yet he isn't here? We want to meet him if he's the one who's really in charge of this operation."

What an opening for a Christian to step into, and Dad walked into it with both feet. "Fellows," he said, "since you've asked, here's your answer. The Lord Jesus Christ is my partner. God has made this business what it is today and I'm proud to be associated with Him."

You can imagine the reaction. Two of the three men were atheistic and the air was soon charged with their rebuttal to such hogwash. With a sneer and a curl of his lips one of them answered, "Come off it, Weston. Cut this religious bit. Every man makes his own way down here. Leave God out of this session." And then, another made the mistake of saying the magic words that gets an athlete sent to the showers by the umpire or coach—he blasphemed, using the Lord's name in his cursing.

Dad's immediate reaction was definite and firm. "Men (*gentlemen* isn't an appropriate term under such conditions), there's the door. It opens out the same way it opened in. This meeting is concluded as of now, and don't ever use those words in my presence again."

The men arose, livid with rage. At the door they shouted, "Weston, you haven't heard the last of this. We'll ruin you and we have the money to do it." Then they slammed the door hard enough to rattle the glass.

Let me tell you, this was just one of the many times I was proud as punch of my Pop. I could understand why those fellows would make a hurried exit because W. G. (my Dad) was riled a mite and he was a big man.

Most folks will remember my father as a very tender, loving, docile, compassionate evangelist, but you

7

see, I knew him back there before he'd mellowed. In his earlier years, he'd been a lumberjack, a rugged mountaineer, and his muscles had muscles. He was all man—a God-fearing, God-loving man.

Wanta hear the end of the story? Sure ya do. Well, it takes a year to tell. During those twelve months, the two multimillionaires who were so mouthy in their declaration against God were bankrupt and the third was well on his way, while my dad's business tripled. Praise the Lord!

You simply can't outdo God. You shovel out to Him and He will shovel back to you, and know this—He has a much bigger shovel!

When I was eleven, I got my first real gun. I'd had BB guns before, and all the cats of the neighborhood hated me because of it, but frankly, I didn't have any *felines* for those critters either. Tsk! Once I heard of a fellow whose pet cat tangled with a steam roller. The newspaper just showed him standing there with a long puss. I haven't anything against those animals mind you, but my preferences are for canines.

But now back to my first shooting iron which Dad bought me. It was a .22 Stevens crack shot rifle and boy, was I ever proud of it. I guess I wanted to be like my dad. As a young man, he was a mountaineer like Daniel Boone and could shoot anything that moved up to a 100 yards and never miss. He was a tremendous athlete in other ways too. He used to pitch baseball for several teams in that old Bald Eagle Valley of Pennsylvania and was just an all-around sportsman. On fishing excursions, no matter where it was, or what type of bait natives of that particular area used, Dad would most always catch the most fish. He never got skunked. He just

8

had a natural knack at outwitting those finny creatures.

My first hunting trip was up in the Allegheny Mountains near Somerset, PA. I stayed with a German family, by the name of Shawlis, right up on top of the ridge. My father first met them on a previous trip which he took with John Himes, a plumber, and John Schneider, a building contractor, old cronies of Dad while he was in the lumber business.

Well, the three of them got lost in the mountains on that occasion. It was cold, close to zero with four to six inches of snow covering the ground. They'd hunted from the crack of dawn until sunset and their hunting coats were loaded down with pheasant, grouse and rabbits as they trudged through the snow. A new blizzard was moving in, making it even more difficult to find their way back to base camp.

Finally, topping a ridge they saw lights in the storm. It was the Shawlis homestead and those gracious, hospitable mountain people invited them in and insisted they stay through the night. They didn't have to insist too hard because they were half frozen and none of the three had had anything to eat all day. They'd tried to munch on a few frozen apples found in a deserted orchard. Their packed lunches and thermos bottles of coffee and hot chocolate were back in that car that had somehow gotten itself lost. So, they were ravenously hungry.

Always in relating the story, John Schneider would chuckle as he'd say, "The bill of fare on the Shawlis table that evening was sauerkraut, and Will"—that was what John called my father—"hated that 'stinking cabbage,' as he called it. But that night, I declare, he ate at least a gallon of the smelly stuff."

Dad would laugh along and add his two-cents' worth, affirming John's story, and saying, "Yep! That, I reckon, was the best food I think I'd ever tasted."

Those who knew my father over the years will verify that sauerkraut was one of his favorite dishes, as can I. During the ten years we traveled together as a father and son evangelistic team, whenever sauerkraut appeared on restaurant menus, it always seemed to find its way to Pop's plate.

Memories crowd in now as I remember my first bicycle, a "Ranger," the finest bike you'd ever want to see, the finest money could buy. That was Dad, so generous with his young'uns. But how quickly we forget those generous moments when we have a childish disagreement. What comes to mind is one very stupid childish experience where my immaturity was showing in plain view.

I got upset one day with Mom and Pop. I felt they were abusing me, didn't understand a fellow's feelings. So, at the ripe old age of twelve, I figured I'd just up and teach them a lesson: I'd run away and break their hearts, that's what I'd do. That would show them they couldn't treat me like they did. Oh, I was in a real huff, you betcha, in a fine fettle to be sure. I told them right out, I did, that I was a-leaving.

I thought they would put up a fuss and get down on their knees and beg me to stay, but do you know what? My dad helped me pack. *My dad helped me pack!* Already my foolproof plans so methodically thought out had sprung a leak. Nothing was panning out the way I had visualized it.

Never will I forget that bleak, dreary, overcast day. Actually, the sun was shining, but not for me it wasn't. They had failed me. My own flesh and blood were turning me out. My parents didn't care a hoot anymore. They wanted me to go! *Oh, woe is me*, I thought. *I might as well go out and eat worms!*

There were all kinds of problems with my plan. In the first place, my timing was wrong. It was evening, in fact, getting dark. I should have planned for an early morning departure. And I hadn't figured on missing supper, so I hadn't packed much food in my bag. Cookies and a baloney sandwich don't quite hack it next to stuffed pork chops, mashed potatoes, corn on the cob and fresh sliced beefsteak tomatoes, with Mom's famous hot apple pie topping that evening's menu.

I never will forget that lonely feeling as I trudged slowly out the back door down those 450 steps—really only five, but it seemed like so many more. I was going extra slow as I was thinking the hesitation waltz might motivate a change of heart on their part. But it wasn't to be. I kept looking back, hoping they'd break the silence in negotiations and recommunicate. Of course, when they did, I was going to be adamant in my stand, and really make them beg for allowing this thing to progress this far.

It wasn't to be. Through the gate and up that winding path alongside the creek I went. It was about a quarter of a mile to the base of the old coal slack dump. What a lonely trek for a twelve-year-old! I can still see the spring water gushing out of that pipe stuck in the hillside. I sat down there to peruse the situation. What had gone wrong? I'd really muffed it. I didn't even have a blanket, or pillow, or matches or anything. Good grief! What a dope!

Then, it got dark—one of those kinds of nights where you can feel the darkness. I started thinking of sneaking back to the house to get those other essentials I'd overlooked. Then suddenly, an old hoot owl concluded my reveries and finalized my decision to scoot for home, and scoot I did, picking my feet up and laying them down, motivated into high gear by that crazy bird's eerie sounds.

At the back screen door I readjusted. I felt I needed to regain my composure, that nonchalance necessary to impress them should I chance to meet any of the household, and have to give an accounting for my sudden reappearance.

I'd been gone about two hours, I guess. But there were no search parties, no notification to the police. In fact, as I crept in, Mom was washing dishes and didn't even look up and I know she'd heard that stupid creaking screen door. But I looked around, and there was my plate, still sitting at my place at the table.

Mom turned then and simply said, "Your supper's still warm. Better eat it before it gets cold."

And thereupon I filled my plate. I wasn't entirely D-double umm-dumb. Sure I ate it. Every bit. Wouldn't you? When I finished, I stacked my dishes on the sink for Mom and walked as unobtrusively as I could toward the stairs. I wanted to get as quickly as possible to the privacy of my room.

That's when Dad stepped out of the sun parlor and said sort of matter-of-factly, "Home so soon?"

Speechless, I gulped, not knowing what to do or say. I was sort of like that fellow who ran his bicycle into a tree; he just laid there speechless and spokeless. I really felt plumb foolish.

Then, with a big smile and hand extended, Dad spoke. "Come here, Son," he said.

And what else could a fellow do but rush into his arms. As he hugged all the huffy feelings away, I just bawled.

"Mom and Dad love you, Bill," he said. "Now you'd better go and hug Mother and thank her for keeping your supper warm. I wanted to put things away, but she said, 'No, he'll be hungry when he gets back,' so I think she rates a little extra hugging."

How could a fellow help but love such super-special people? The rebellion was crushed; they'd won the day. How wise they are, I thought later, as I lay on my bed reliving the past few hours. I suddenly saw how immature my actions were and was so ashamed of myself for even thinking of ever leaving such a mom and pop.

I learned my lesson well, I did. After that, when I'd see bratty kids yammering for their own way I'd think, "Shut up, you spoiled young'un. You're lucky your parents don't leave you and your go-cart in some tow-away zone."

That makes me think of the little tyke who was carrying his little suitcase around and around the block. When asked what he was doing, he replied, "I'm running away from home." The questioner smiled and said, "Yes, but you are just walking around and around the same block." To which our little runaway responded, "Sure, 'cause I'm not allowed to cross the street."

Dad's Growing Up Years

Some of the most fun times of my life were those occasions when our family would sit around the supper table and listen as Dad would regale us with tales from his youth. A mountain lad, he was raised in a log cabin at the foot of the Allegheny Mountain Range between Phillipsburg and Port Matilda, PA. Let me cite a few of those stories here that I never wearied of hearing.

One time, as a thirteen-year-old, Dad was told by his father to get his two-wheeler and hustle into Port Matilda to the general store to pick up a shearing pin for the farm tractor. The urgency of the request, coupled with the words, "Get a move on now," caused my Dad to neglect getting his pants' guard.

Pumping that old bike for all it was worth, he crested a hill. From there it was all downgrade into Port. Picking up speed, his one trouser leg caught in the sprocket of his bike which rapidly but surely produced a catastrophe with disastrous results. The only shoulder strap on his jeans popped and his pants were wound down to his ankles quicker than a lizard can scamper across a hot rock.

He and the bike rolled into the ditch. He was hurt, too, with cuts to his right leg that had blood streaming down. But the biggest hurt of all was the embarrassment the accident caused. Jockey shorts were a luxury unheard of by those mountain boys. The upper part of his torso was still covered by an old hickory-colored shirt, but the lower extremities were. . . . Well, you could say he was sure caught unawares.

As I said, he was hurt, but worst of all he was tied down tight by tangled britches threaded in a sprocket and couldn't extricate himself from said predicament. And wouldn't you know it, the place in the ditch that embraced him and the bicycle was right in front of the home of a maiden lady. She was one of the town's characters, a wee bit tetched. You could say the tower was there, but her bell was missing.

She'd been a sitting on her front porch and saw the whole thing happen. Sizing up the situation, which I might add for her took a spell, she finally came a shuffling onto the scene with her shears and began to cut my daddy loose.

What a plight! And to make things more frustrating, she'd cut a spell and then roll over and laugh and laugh. Before long she got him cut free and Dad, blushing like a new spring sunrise, scrambled out of that ditch and headed for the protective cover of the forest and made tracks for home. As he came out of the woods and across the barnyard clearing to the cabin, his mom came out of the door, looked, gasped in disbelief, took another gander and said, "Land sakes, Billy, what in the world happened to you?"

Dad said usually his mother could heal all ills, but this was no place nor time for reply. The first thing on his agenda was the privacy of his room and another pair of jeans.

By the way, that maiden lady got her comeuppance. A contortionist, in town with a cure-all medicine show, told those country folks that one bottle of his elixir would enable them to do what he could do. So saying, he proceeded to wrap both legs around his neck. Folks are so gullible. They must have read Gullible's Travels, I reckon. Anyhow, several bought that bottled liquid, among them our aforementioned shears-and-laugh-and-tumble friend.

One day, a few weeks later, when the egg man came by to pick up the eggs she gathered daily from her little chicken farm, his knock on the front door went unanswered. Going around to the back door, he heard through the screen, someone groaning and a weak voice plaintively calling, "Oh, somebody please help me."

Entering the house, he discovered our maiden lady sprawled on her living room floor. Yes, you guessed it. The bottle was empty. And she had managed somehow to get one leg up and around her neck and couldn't get it back down. Suffice it to say, the resultant problem, both in embarrassment and excruciating pain, sort of cooled off her enthusiasm for relating to others the bike-and-scissors story.

You've heard the old cliché, "Chickens come home to roost" and the "idle hands" bit also, I'm sure. Dad's brother, Victor, had caught a rather bad cold and so my angelic father decided he would help his very busy mother by preparing her springtime tonic—her cure for her family's ailing times. I remember Dad saying, "I had more fun and would rather see one of my brothers have to take that dose than to go to a Sunday school picnic!"

So, securing the hog's lard, saltpeter, molasses, castor oil and several other choice ingredients, he combined same in a bowl, and noticing his stirring finger was pretty dirty, applied same in the procedure until it came out nice and clean. Then, sweet little kid that he was with his halo polished and shining, he brought that conglomeration to his mama and so piously said, "Mom, Victor's been awful sick 'n knowing you've been so busy, I've fixed the medicine for ya, 'n all ya gotta do is give it to him."

Do you want to know something that's for sure? My grandma was gifted with the wisdom of Solomon. With a twinkle in her eye she said, "That's awfully nice and thoughtful of you Billy, but I've noticed you, too, have had a hackin' cough of late." And before my dad could shed his present surroundings, my grandma had him on the floor. Astride of him, she held his nose and poured that whole mess down his gullet. Wheweee! Now don't we learn our lessons the hard way?

Stuart was one of Dad's older brothers. He was a wiry, rugged man of the forest and had a farm up there in the mountains. What he loved most was to trap or hunt game. He could imitate the calls of a turkey, owl, wildcat and others to perfection.

As a young fellow he'd been courting a mountain gal and was a mite jealous of her attentions being displayed toward any other buck in that area. My dad, in telling this incident, intimated she really wasn't much to look at. In fact she was rather frumpy in appearance with what I'd describe as a supreme court figure—no appeal. Stuart, though, thought she was a dream boat. Of course, there's no accounting for a fellow's tastes when that amoral bug bites you. Love is blind—we all know that. Dream boat? From Dad's description 'n with my imagination, I kinda figured her cargo had shifted, 'n most likely, if Moses coulda seen her, he'd have passed another law!

Anyhow, one evening a drummer—the title given to a salesman of that day and time—tried to cut in on Stuart's territory. He went to see Stuart's girl on top of the mountain. Stuart found out and was furious. He decided he'd fix that sales guy, maybe teach him a lesson that would permanently separate him from that general area for good. So late one night, as that city fellow was cautiously maneuvering his way over roots 'n rocks down that steep mountain trail, Stuart hid himself over in the dense laurel bushes beside that path. As the salesman got close, Stuart suddenly let loose with a blood curdling wildcat scream, while violently rustling the bushes.

Well, as later he told it to the Weston clan, that city fellow had been singing "Nearer My God To Thee" to bolster his morale down that darkened trail. When he heard that scream and awful racket in the brush, he thought his time had come. The last note of his song ended on the lost chord and with wings sproutin' on his feet like the Greek god Mercury, he took off at speeds that Stuart 'clared would've established world records for short and long distances. Suffice it to say, he didn't put in a reappearance to that gal's abode.

Come to think of it, Dad said, Stuart, too, must've gotten a good look at her in broad daylight 'cause he didn't climb that hill anymore either. Reckon he had better things to do with his time—like the occasion when he got his other brothers involved in a calf and cat caper.

Tying one of the farm's toms to a young steer's tail will make for more excitement than you can possibly imagine. With that calf bawling and the cat screeching like a banshee while clambering and clawing that steer's buttocks, the whole side of that mountain echoed and reechoed. Fences, barbed or otherwise, were no deterrent. By the time that steer was finally shed of that feline, he had torn up quite a bit of property.

On that occasion my grandpa's belt left his britches, and the boys, including my dad, lined up for a patriotic whoop-de-doo, as their pa led the parade to the tune of the "Stars and Stripes Forever." They saw the stars, and he provided the stripes.

One day in early spring, the hogs were a-wallerin' and one had gotten itself real comfy right in the middle of the lane in its own private mud hole, if you please. Over time, it had wriggled down into the mud until its back was level with the road. Around that time, another drummer, a real city slicker, was plying his trade in that community. He had sold Grandpa some farm equipment. On that particular day, work was pretty well over. With the chores completed for the moment, all the boys were a-lollygagging on the front porch and steps. Several were chewing on straw stubble as they watched each other taking turns riding the family's one bicycle up and down the lane. But, mind you, not past that old sow–they knew better.

The city fellow came out of the house where he'd been talking to Dad's pa and stood watching the fellas and their bike riding antics for a spell. Suddenly, inspired I reckon, 'n seeing that pig sprawled level with the lane's roadbed, he said, "Here, let me show you fellows some real bicycle riding. You see that ol' pig down there? Well, I betcha I can ride over her afore she can get up outta that mudhole."

Well now, right away the boys all tried to convince him not to try such foolishness. They assured him that no one could ride that fast or complete such a trick. But he pooh-poohed their warnings and bragging further as to his skills in bike riding, he said, "Think it can't be done, eh? Well, I'll just show ya."

So the boys, their warnings unheeded, settled down to watch the proceedings. Going to the top of the lane to get up more speed, he hollered, "Here she goes!" And down that lane he came. Yep! He was a pretty fair bike rider all right. The boys all concurred on that. But city fellow that he was, he didn't rightly know pigs and their lightning coordination when attacked by a two-wheeler. Oh me! When that front tire hit that ol' sow's back, she rose up squealing like the rapture had taken place. The bike went one way and that poor guy was launched into space. It was the first orbit shot, I think. My uncles ran to pick him up. Though busted up a mite, luckily he'd been thrown into another sow-sized wallow and the depth of water and mud had somewhat broken his impact with terra firma.

The moral of this tale, I think, is clearly understood. We're not "porking" fun at city people, mind you, but don't ever try to out hustle an ol' sow under similar circumstances 'cause you'll always wind up second best.

Following about five or six such tales, Dad would then say, "It's getting late," and I'd think, *Shucks! How I wish time would stand still.* I could have listened all night to my dad's storytelling. Yep! Back then folks made their own fun times. How I wish I could relive those wonderful years. Families were families then, with no TV to distract from just good old-fashioned fun sessions. Talk, laughter, fellowship—topped so many times with Mom's home-made ice cream. We'd all had a hand in cranking that old freezer, chucking in the snow or crushed iced. Boy, it was good. I think the key was that rich, pure milk and cream, the kind that got so thick you had to spoon it out of the bottle. Pray tell, when did you last see a bottle of milk with thick cream on the top? Today I think cows, when they see milk trucks roll by with signs like "pasteurized," "homogenized" and all the rest, must sigh and "Mooooo," which interpreted would say, "Man, do we ever feel inadequate!"

Following those glorious evenings together as a family, we would always bow or kneel for family prayers before we headed for bed. One by one, Dad would pray for each member of the household, committing us to God's care. Oh my! What families have missed in never sharing in a time like that! Yes, I lived in a home, not a house. A home is a place where there's love and warmth, understanding and communication with one another. A house is just a place to change clothes before you go out for the evening. Today it's TV dinners. Makes a fellow wonder if Home Economics is still being taught in the schools or if it's just a course in advanced thawing!

And today's entertainment, TV—everyone is glued to the boob tube. Someone sagely said, "We have more TVs in America today than bathtubs, and that's a dirty shame." I heard statistics recently that there were 60 million TV sets and only 40 million bathtubs. If that's so it appears there are 20 million dirty Americans looking at the tube.

We eat in shifts now. Everybody's moonlighting, it seems. The first shift arises at 5 a.m. Menu: burnt toast and coffee, then off and away. The second shift, hearing the first shift's alarm clock at the crack of dawn, stuffs the crack and goes back to nod land until aroused again at 7. The last shift usually drags down about a quarter to 12. Same menu, then off and away.

About 8 p.m., the fashionable time for dinner today—in the old days, that was three hours late—folks converge again on the house. They holler "hi," to all they chance to meet, grab a quick snack, change clothes and zip off again for the bright lights—cinema, discos or some other entertainment. About midnight the kids get in. They have school, you see, and need a few hours shuteye. Out of habit, they pull the button on the tube. Ugh! Another repeat program, so it's off to bed.

About 1:30 or 2 a.m., Mom and Dad come dragging in.

Janie calls down, "Is that you, Mom and Dad?"

"Yes."

"OK, but don't lock the front door 'cause Grandma's not in yet."

Grandpa Woodring, Mom's dad, owned the hotel in that bustling little metropolis of Port Matilda. Aunt Mary Pringle and Uncle Chester ran the corner drug store. Uncle Charlie and Aunt Amy managed the bank. A general store and post office combined occupied the other corner of that plot of ground that made up that particular main street U.S.A. The highway down the Bald Eagle Valley between Altoona and Bellefonte ran right through the center of town. Grandpa Woodring was also the mayor of this thriving community and therefore the overseer of the park management where all the family reunions and town picnics took place.

It's always interesting to hear how folks get together. I mean girls and their beaus. Dad met Tessie Woodring, my mom, at one of those town picnics. She crossed his line of vision and somehow or other got stuck in his eye. You could say he suffered from an im*pair*ment in his vision, a common malady that is only cured by holding hands under a full moon.

Well, Tessie's long brown curly tresses, pretty face and mincing walk caused Will's heartstrings to twang and boing! The damage was done. Anybody who thinks it isn't fun to fall in love sure needs their battery recharged. How I loved to hear Mom and Dad give their accounts of their courting days. Like so many, they'd correct each other's stories as to certain happenings and who was the aggressor on occasions. It was so wholesome, so refreshingly different from today's 20th-century pattern. How I'd laugh as they'd relate their dating problems—trying to find ways to be alone, shed of prying eyes, as chaperones in those times were very much in vogue. Today's world would ask, "Chaperones? What in the world were they?" Well, to reply, usually they were people who never quite made the team, but were in there intercepting the passes.

Anyhow, when my Grandpa Woodring would come to visit us I'd get Mom or Dad to tell of the times when Grandpa would bang on the stove pipe that ran from the parlor downstairs up through his bedroom to inform Will it was time to cease tarrying with his daughter Tessie. You all know how saying goodnight to your best gal is a custom of long standing. You stand there a looooonng time. Tsk!

I liked to watch all of their faces during the telling of that particular story. Dad's teasing of Mom's reactions to what she thought was her father's rude insistence that her young man must depart when it was only 9:30 p.m. My grandpa would grin kinda sheepishly and say, "Well, hittin' that ol' stove pipe always got results." And then he'd win the day by adding, "You couldn't have gotten a better man, Tessie, than Will." Mom 'n' Dad would look at each other lovingly, squeeze hands and little me, looking on, would silently say, "Amen."

Yes, obedience to parent's wishes was a way of life then. Children of all ages, as long as they still resided at home, knew respect for and obedience to the laws of said abode were to be done without murmuring or questioning. If you didn't adhere, you were most liable to get rubbed down with hickory oil. This substance oozed from a sprout, about an arm's-length long, taken from a hickory tree. When vigorously applied to the back of one's front, it usually made a feller's rememberer become quite keen and caused him to much prefer obedience over chastisement.

Yep, back then, if you wanted to avoid a visit to the woodshed, you were mighty careful about smarting off or giving any lip to your elders. They

25

were the law, and court sessions had no delays, appeals or changes of venue. But I've discovered since, real love motivated their actions. When I became a father myself, I found the answer to a statement my parents used to make that thoroughly confused me—"This hurts me more than it does you." As a kid, with my buttocks burning, I never could figure how adults could lie like that and still have the nerve ta whup me for what I figured was much less sinful than their fibbing. Today the voices of Mom and Pop are silenced, but I understand about those whupping sessions. They loved me. I'm so sure of that now.

CHAPTER THREE

Escape from the Shadow of Death: Dad's Life Story

In the early 1960s Dad was in a meeting with his dear pastor friend, Rev. Joe Nelson, in High Point, North Carolina. As was his custom, Dad would give his life story on the closing night of such a series of meetings. Following a brief introduction by Brother Nelson that Sunday evening, my father gave his testimony. Based on a tape recording of that service, it is presented here as given except where edited for length and clarity.

I've been in God's seminary now for over thirty-six years and I'm going to stay in school until the Lord comes. My education before that time was for the purpose of attaining success in the business world. Now I'm seeking to learn how to bring God down to meet the hearts of men and women, boys and girls.

Psalm 30:1-4 provides a scriptural background to the story of God's dealings in my life:

> I will extol thee, O LORD; for thou hast lifted me up, and hast not made my foes to rejoice over me.

O LORD my God, I cried unto thee, and thou hast healed me.

O LORD, thou hast brought up my soul from the grave: thou hast kept me alive, that I should not go down to the pit.

Sing unto the LORD, O ye saints of his, and give thanks at the remembrance of his holiness. (Psalm 30:1-4)

My text for the evening is Jeremiah 33:3: "Call unto me, and I will answer thee, and shew thee great and mighty things, which thou knowest not." This is God's voice to all of our hearts.

I've dedicated this testimony to the memory of a little mountain mother who first dedicated me to God before I was born. I'm the seventh child of the family and since mother, due to her time in life, knew I'd be her last child, her heart was burdened that she might have a son that would preach the gospel. I do not know how long she waited alone before the Lord in that old log house, but she gave me into His keeping before I came into this world. And the Lord assured her that the child she was to bear would honor Him by giving forth this old story of redeeming love. My mother never heard me preach a sermon, but she died believing God would keep His word, His promise to her, and that's why I'm here—God's word cannot be broken.

I'm sure the Lord has told her up in glory that her prayer was answered and one day, perhaps very soon we shall meet and I can tell her myself. But I long to see my Savior first of all for I owe everything to Him.

I've thanked God so many times for a mother who gave me back to God before I was born. How wonderful it would be if every child would be given to Him before they arrived. If they were, we wouldn't have this awful condition that exists in our world today.

My mother received me into her arms, watched over me when I did not know how to do anything for myself. She told me after I was old enough to understand, that from the time I was born it seemed like the old enemy was determined to kill me. But, when others would give me up, due to some mishap or illness, she'd just wait on God and remind Him of His promise and the Lord would spare my life.

On one occasion, she told me how when I was just a wee child, she was in the old log cabin alone. Our neighbor had been having some mental problems. He lived on an adjoining farm about one-half mile away. One day, he suddenly went violently insane and burst into our home with a heavy pick handle. Raising it to strike, he said he had come to kill her and the baby and he would give her just one minute to live.

Now one minute isn't very long, but one minute with God can change everything. She said she looked up into the face of that mad man and she couldn't utter a sound. She was speechless. He held that weapon over her defenseless head and there seemed no way of escape. In her heart, however, there was a mighty cry that went up to our Father in heaven. She said, "I reminded Him that the little one I held in my arms would honor Him and that this awful thing just could not be."

The mad man still stood there frothing at the mouth, but he couldn't strike. He was absolutely powerless to hurt my mother or her baby. And soon after, the men of the neighborhood, who were supposed to have watched over him, came in and led him away. He later died in the insane asylum, a raving maniac. God had heard a prayer that man couldn't hear.

Sometimes you may not be able to voice your petition, but friend, God Almighty knows your heart. Aren't you glad for that? He can hear what man cannot hear. He sees what man cannot see and He's always able and willing to meet us.

I thank the Lord for my Christian heritage. I had a praying father and mother, and oh, how I wish every boy and girl could be raised in a home where the family prayed together. But there comes a time in our lives when we must call on God for our own needs. It becomes a personal matter. While I was raised around a family altar and brought up under the atmosphere of prayer, it was as a teenager in an old-fashioned meeting that I discovered I had never invited Christ to come into my heart as my personal Savior. It was then that I really called on God for the first time and I asked Jesus to come into my heart.

I find many times this is true. Folks are brought up in a Christian home, attend Sunday school and church, and yet have neglected to call upon the Lord to receive God's Son. They might have religion, but they have never had that personal contact and relationship with the Lord Jesus Christ.

We didn't call it "revival" back there in the mountains. They called it "big meeting." Those old-fashioned mountain folks believed they could pray revival blessing down on the whole community. And so, at least once a year, they'd determine to have these Big Meetings and God Almighty honored their faith.

They didn't have an evangelist. In fact, I had never met an evangelist until I was pretty well grown up. But they did have an old-fashioned mountain preacher. He had five charges where he walked sometimes as much as seventeen to eighteen miles on a Sunday. He would pour his heart out preaching the gospel. He didn't know much about the things of this world and he never had gone to seminary because he hadn't had that opportunity. But he'd waited on God and was born of the Spirit and filled with the Spirit. He knew that people were lost and he knew that the blood of Christ was the only remedy for sin. And if you know that, you can be a blessing to folks.

He would pour out his heart and God would honor the Word and come down and bless. Then, when he'd gotten the folks started, he'd move on to another place and they'd carry on the meeting by themselves. And sometimes those meetings would last seven or eight weeks and nobody played out. God would come down and save folks all over the community.

Friends, I'd like to see one more Big Meeting before Jesus comes, wouldn't you? Just an old-fashioned outpouring of God, prayed down by people who still believe that God answers prayer. And I thank God He does.

It was in one of those Big Meetings I heard the call of God to my heart and I slipped down with others to an old-fashioned mourners' bench. We didn't have an altar or a platform in the church there. We didn't even have any musical instruments. It wasn't because we were against them; we just didn't have any money to buy them.

As far as music was concerned, we had an old fellow with a pitch pipe. He pitched and we piped, and the dear Lord put up with it and we got blessed, so I guess it was all right.

At any rate I came down to that old mourners' bench. It was a place where people came and really cried their hearts out to God because they'd sinned. And in those meetings if folks didn't get through one night, they came back again and they stayed at it until they did find peace with God. It's not how long you're down, but what you have when you get up that counts.

I was kneeling there, seeking the Lord the best I could as a teenage mountain boy, when a dear old man came along. He laid his hand on my head and said, "Listen, my boy, Jesus said, 'He that cometh unto me I will in nowise cast out.'" And, you know, somehow the Lord blessed that word to my heart. I can't tell you how it happened, but Jesus came into my heart and I knew I was saved and had no more business at the mourners' bench. The first person I wanted to tell was my mother.

Now in that meeting, it was different from any other place I've ever been. As soon as the meeting would start, folks that loved the Lord with all their heart would leave their seats and come up around in back of the mourners' bench and spend the evening there. They sang the hymns, exhorted or prayed and when people came down, they didn't come to a lonely bench. There were folks there to pray with them. And when they had met God, there was an old-fashioned reception committee to welcome them into the family of God. Those dear mountain folk really loved to see folk come to get saved and I think that's the way we ought to be today. We ought to love to see folks come to Jesus, to receive Him.

Well, my mother was with that group. And I ran around the bench to tell her that Jesus had come into my heart. She just took me in her arms and the tears flowed down her cheeks. She wasn't sorry; she was happy!

Mother was different from my father in her reactions. I had an old-fashioned shouting Methodist for a daddy. I think he would have scared some of us modern folks out of the meetings. He used to get happy around the family altar. We'd read the Word of God and pray and the Lord would fill his soul, and he'd just fill up to his mouth and he'd let go. Sometimes it came so sudden I'd nearly jump over my chair.

Now, my mother, she was different. She was a quiet little soul and she'd just keep her mouth shut, fill up to her eyes and it ran down her cheeks. It was the same Lord, but His blessings work out differently in different people. But one thing is for sure—when He gets inside with His blessings they're going to come out. You'll know something has happened in your heart and so will others. Even the old cat and the dog will notice the difference in your attitudes.

I'll never forget the next morning. The old farm didn't look the same. I remember going down to do the chores that morning. Why it seemed like even the old hens were glad I got saved. They cackled around so nice and I felt so good I gave them some extra corn. Then it came time to milk the cow and that was one chore I despised. We had just one cow and she never did give too much milk and she was stingy about what she did give. I had to pull it out of her. And while I was milking her, she seemed to delight in wrapping her burr-filled tail around my neck. I didn't like that cow one bit! But I can tell you that the morning after Jesus saved me, that old cow looked so good I could have kissed her.

Had something changed the farm and the cow and the chickens? No, they were the same, but sunshine had come into my heart, and that's the only cure for the world's troubles in any hour. We'll never legislate righteousness and we'll never have peace in this world until the Prince of Peace comes. And you'll never know what real peace is until the Lord Jesus Christ brings His peace and cleansing into your heart. That's the peace that the world can never give and, thank God, they cannot take it away. If we lose it, it's because we've cast it away through our own disobedience.

Well, I had a good time serving God as I was growing up. How quickly the years slipped by. Then one day when mother thought I was old enough to understand, she took me aside and told me about my dedication ceremony. She hadn't even told my father. She had kept it as a secret between her and the Lord.

She was real proud that day when she told me, "Son, some day you are going to preach." She thought I'd be thrilled, but I disappointed her because I wasn't.

I looked her in the face and said, "Mother, I love the Lord and I sure want to go to heaven when I die, but I'll never preach."

She asked, "Well Son, why wouldn't you want to preach?"

I said, "Because our preacher's just as poor as we are and we ain't got nothing."

We were poor back there in the mountains. They used to talk about being as poor as Job's turkey. One old fellow, when they asked him how poor he thought that was, replied, "It was so poor it had to lean up against the fence to gobble." I don't know about that, but I know we were poor. My father was broken down. He had been severely wounded in the Civil War, and my mother had also suffered when she was a child. Somebody had dropped her when she was a baby. She grew up with a hump on her back. She and dad brought several children into the world and we were all desperately poor as far as things were concerned.

We had neighbors who had everything. They made fun of me. They called me that poor Weston kid. They didn't want to play with me because my clothes were old and pretty shabby. That boy Joseph in the Bible never had anything on me. He had a coat of many colors, but I had coats and pants both of many colors. When your mother tries to dress you up in hand-me-down clothes that five other brothers have outgrown, you come out looking pretty much like a crazy quilt. Yes, we were very poor, but we were honest. Though my daddy and my mother did the best they could, I was sick and tired of being laughed at.

When I said that, my mother began to cry and I'll confess I did a little bawling myself. But I said, "Mother, no use fussing, because I just won't ever preach. I'm going to be a business man and someday you're gonna have things like other mothers have. You've never had anything and I've never had anything, and I'm just tired being made fun of."

As I said this, I was thinking of that old preacher of ours—his pants were patched both front and back. And all I could see for my whole lifetime was wearing patched pants and patched clothes and I'd had enough of it. So I rebelled against the Lord that day, and I lost all the peace and joy out of my heart.

My mother's reply was simple: "Billy, we may not have things like others, but Son, we do have Jesus. And if we got all the things in the world and it cost us our Lord, it wouldn't be worth it."

She was so right. But I was determined to have my own way and like so many others I had to pay the price for it. I educated myself, working back there in the mountains. For a number of years I taught school. Over time, I worked my way through business college and finally was prepared to face the world as an architect and homebuilder, the profession I had chosen. A lovely girl in the community had consented to go through life with me and so I was ready to leave the old farm.

My mother never nagged me, but she prayed for me constantly. Sometimes when we were alone, she'd slip her arms around me and speak a few words to me in love. On this occasion she took me aside and said, "Billy [she always called me Billy], you're going to leave the old farm and follow the profession in life that you've chosen, and it seems wonderful to you, but you know it's not God's will for your life, and you're gonna have a lot of heartaches and trouble, but someday, boy, you're going to preach." Then she smiled right in my face.

I said, "All right mother, if that's the way you feel about it, okay." But I had no thought of ever following the Lord in that ministry. I was determined more than ever to have my own way.

After my wife and I were married, we moved into the Pittsburgh area and began life at the bottom because there wasn't any other place to begin. We settled down in a little Westinghouse community where they were building a large factory. We thought it would be a very fine place and a good opportunity for the type of business in which I hoped to get started.

However, things became very difficult. There were days of great depression and struggle. Every time we were climbing the ladder of success, something would happen and we'd be back down at the bottom again. We followed two of our babies to the cemetery. Bitterness filled my heart. I blamed God for my troubles like a great many other folk do.

There was only one church in the area, a community church, and that's where we went. Looking back, I'm quite certain the pastor there didn't know what it was to be born again. He was a good mixer, a great fellow as far as a social program was concerned, and he was surrounded by a group of very fine people, but their program was social. I don't think they'd ever known anything about old-time revivals. He came to our home and persuaded my wife and me to join his church. I did have grace enough to tell him I wasn't fit to join his church, but he looked me right in the eye and said, "Well, Weston, you're as good as my other men."

Well now, I agreed with that, because I knew the type of men he had. I'd been out with them. But that didn't excuse me. But you see, I may as well be honest with you, I was thinking it would probably help me in my business to join the church and have these social contacts. So, I joined and played church. And I'm afraid today there are a good many people in our country just like that—playing church.

I did love young people. I always have and I always will. I had always been interested in them and so, to do my part in that church, I gathered around me a large group of splendid young people. Young couples were moving into that new housing area by the hundreds. So I had a wonderful group of these young folks in my Sunday school class. We had lots of parties and good social times together, but I wasn't any help to them spiritually. Why? Because I'd lost all the joy and peace out of my own heart. I tried to make up for it by showing them a good time socially. Now there's nothing wrong with God's people having fun, but if that's all they're having then they ought to change their name, for after all, the church was instituted that people might find peace and shelter under the blood of Christ and then be encouraged to grow in the Christian faith.

I learned my lesson the hard way. You don't fool young people very long. You may think you do, but you don't. They know what kind of person you are. We were out one evening for one of our social gatherings. The girls were preparing the refreshments that were to be served and I went over to see how they were getting along. I heard my name mentioned and I thought I'd hear something nice about myself so I slipped behind the portiere and listened. I really got an earful.

That young lady was very earnest as she said, "Yes, girls, I like Mr. Weston. He does the best he can for us; but if I were in trouble, if I were sick or if I were dying, I wouldn't want that fellow around." There was utter disgust in her voice.

I stood there in deep thought. She wouldn't want me around because I've lost everything that is of value in an hour of need. I knew that back when I was a teenager, if she'd been in trouble, I could've prayed with her and helped her, but now, she wouldn't want me around. Again it hit me, I don't have what folks need when they're in trouble. Well, God smote my heart that evening, smote it very deeply. Of course, Mother was praying and she had her friends also praying for me.

About that time our town decided to have a union evangelistic campaign. Churches had been springing up over the area so there was enough interest to plan such a meeting. And, of all the things, they elected me chairman to head up the arrangements for the campaign.

I wrote my mother and told her we were going to have a meeting, and she wrote back and said, "If you're going to have a Big Meeting, you send for my preacher, Rev. E.G. Sawyer. He will do you good."

We had rented a new building that was destined later to be a garage. With the rented chairs and platform erected we had a fine auditorium that would seat about 800 people. We engaged an evangelist and had our musical program arranged. Then, shortly before the meetings were to begin, our evangelist said he would be unable to come. So, the committee suggested I get in touch with my mother's preacher. I did and he was a very gracious fellow and said he would come.

I'm sure the Lord was in it, for he was a true man of God, a man that had power both with God and with men. He was an eloquent, master preacher. The first night that auditorium was packed. They surely did turn out for that opening service of the crusade. I introduced mother's preacher. He got up, opened the word of God, came right down the line, exposing sin and exalting Jesus Christ as the Savior of mankind. And I thought I was the only person in that building that he was preaching to.

It's wonderful to let God get you into a corner and really talk to your own heart. So many times folks come to church and pass the message off, saying, "Oh, how I wish my neighbors were here. It's just what they need." Let's not mind the neighbor. Let God witness and talk to our own hearts. He spoke that night to mine. I was under deep conviction.

We had put a eighty-foot bench at the front as a place to pray, but during those opening days there wasn't even a hand raised for prayer. However, I was getting under such deep conviction, I couldn't eat or sleep. And the prayer of my heart today is that we might again see folks so moved by God that they can't enjoy any of these things until they repent and get right with the Lord. We need old-time conviction again in America. We need some old-time gospel preaching that causes folks to again fear grieving the Almighty.

Well, Sawyer was an old-fashioned preacher, and
God honored His Word. I finally got to the place
where I couldn't stand it any longer, so I went up to
see him. I found him on his face before God because he wasn't used to having that kind of meeting. He'd seen hundreds of people saved,
responding to his ministry of the word in other
places, and here, he hadn't even seen a hand raised
for prayer.

When he finished praying, he looked up and I
was standing there waiting. He said, "Well, Weston
what can I do for you?"

"Mr. Sawyer, I came up to get right with God."

He looked me right in the eye and said, "It's
about time, you poor miserable hypocrite."

His bluntness shocked me, but you know he was
right.

Then he followed up with, "Your mother has
been praying for you. You've been running away
from God and His will for your life. You're playing
at religion. It's not religion but Christ you need and
with whom you need to get aligned. You are not living like a Bible Christian and you know it."

I knew he was telling me the truth about myself
and the church. If folks all over this country pro-
fessing Christ would live like a Bible Christian we
could have old-time revival all over this nation. My,
how God would meet us and bless this great land of
ours!

Well, I looked at him and I said, "Sawyer, I don't
need any more preaching. I failed God back there in
my younger life because I was sick of being made
fun of. I rebelled against the Lord, and I've never really been happy. I've put up a front, and yes, played

41

church if you want to put it like that. I've tried to find a little release by being kind to young people, but I've never been happy. God knows how far I've gotten away from Him, so I came up here to get right with the Lord."

He said, "All right, but not here. You're chairman of this meeting. Tonight, when I'm through preaching, you get up and tell them who you are and then get down at that old bench and stay there until you find peace with God."

"Now, Sawyer," I said, "I couldn't do that. You ought to recognize that. I'm chairman of this meeting. Everybody knows me. To do that would kill me."

"Well, you may as well be dead," he said, "because you're no good anyhow."

I'd met a man who loved my soul more than my friendship. Any preacher who will stand behind the sacred desk and make people feel they are right when they are wrong is not your friend. Your friend is the man who will preach the Word. If we're not living right, God will then speak to us, convict us by His Spirit, and we can repent and get right. Men who will help us get back to God is what we need throughout the world today; men who will stand by the Book and with tender hearts love the people, but be fearless in proclaiming the truth found in His Word.

Well, that night, when he was through, Sawyer turned, looked right at me and said, "All right, Weston, it's your turn."

There were all my friends, business associates, my Sunday school class, lawyers, doctors, those I had been running with, living worldly. Somehow,

God gave me the strength to stand before that audience. I told them that as a teenager I'd given my heart to Christ, but that I'd sinned, rebelled against God, determined to have my own way. I said I hadn't had a happy day since, and that I didn't care what anybody else was going to do, I was going to get right with God. I then made my way down from that platform to that lonely old bench and sought God with all my heart.

I want you to know, God really met me! He cleansed my heart from all my backsliding. When I finally looked up, through my tears, that old bench was filled from one end to the other. God had broken through and in the next two weeks we had over 700 men and women and young people seek the Lord for salvation. It was a marvelous moving of God that changed the entire life of our community. Folks' language changed. Instead of oaths, now you heard greetings in the name of the Lord, even on the streets. Almost my entire Sunday school class came to know Christ in those meetings and my, what a time we now had in our fellowship sessions! We didn't play church anymore. We continued with old-fashioned revival in our Sunday school and that's the way it ought to be.

What a change in the atmosphere of our community! It was truly wonderful. Our pastor was gloriously saved and we had such wonderful cooperation and fellowship in all the churches. And everybody loved everybody else no matter what their denominational affiliation. Wouldn't it be great if again this spirit prevailed throughout our land? How my heart cries out that this great country of ours might again return to the simple faith and trust in God that filled the hearts of our forefathers, the kind that prompted them to seek Divine counsel and wisdom for the solving of our national problems.

Anyhow, it was about as near heaven around there for those years as I've ever known. But then, World War 1 broke out and the young men from my Sunday school class began to leave to enter the service of our country. Their letters came back telling of the conditions and the need of God in those army camps and my heart went out to those servicemen.

One day my wife looked across the table as my mind was preoccupied, thinking of those lads out there. Some already had gone overseas. As I sat there playing with my food, she said, "Husband, I know what's wrong with you. Your heart is with your boys and if you feel you could help them, I can take care of the babies."

Bless her heart. She's always been like that. With me being an evangelist, we haven't lived too much together these past thirty-six years, but I know she's home praying for me. We love each other, I think, as much as any two people can love each other.

Recently, one lady said to my wife in my daughter's hearing, "You know, Mrs. Weston, I wouldn't want a husband like yours, being away like he is all the time." And my daughter, Bea, told me, "Daddy, Mother just smiled and replied, 'Well, for your information, I'd rather have him part time, than any other man I know of full time in this world.' " That helped me.

We've been together nearly sixty years and it's grown sweeter as the years go by. It was never her fault if we didn't have victory in our home. It was always my fault; and, men, if you're having problems at home and it's your fault, for Jesus' sake and your family's sake get right with God and serve Him with all your heart. He can give you a united home. It means everything!

I had eighteen months with the boys in that struggle. God helped me and I had the privilege of leading many a homesick boy to Christ. Some of them went overseas and never came back, but I'm sure I'm going to meet them in heaven some day.

When that war was over and I was released, I came back with a burden on my heart to go into full-time service for my Lord, but I had a family to take care of and I didn't have any money. During a long prayer meeting, I promised the Lord if He would help me make some money so I could take care of mother and the babies, I'd do anything He wanted me to do. And I meant it in my heart.

God answered that prayer in a most remarkable way and that lumber company in the Pittsburgh area still stands to this day, in witness to that fact. I severed all connections with the business world when my health broke down, so I no longer have any interests in that West Elizabeth, PA Lumber & Supply Company. But God truly heard and answered my prayer.

Then again, I'm sorry to say, I failed Him, but not this time because of rebellion, but because the enemy deceived me. I had money and the Lord was prospering me just as I had asked Him to do. Into this success the devil came and so subtly said, "Your mother just didn't understand God's program. What the Lord wants is for you to continue in business and pour your money into the church treasury and pay other young men who are trained to preach, and in that way you'll be fulfilling your mother's dedication. You'll thus be preaching the gospel through several ministries."

And, of course, that sounded very plausible, very, very reasonable. All this reasoning came in my mind directly from the enemy, and believe me he's on the trail of everyone, trying first of all to keep you from accepting Christ, and then, after you've accepted Him, to keep you out of the center of His will, to defeat your life. That's Satan's business—to kill, steal and destroy.

My mistake, in listening to such reasoning, was that I forgot that my mother didn't dedicate money because she didn't have any money. She dedicated a boy, her son, to God. So I tried to substitute money for a life and you can't do that. You know, after all, you and I didn't bring any money into this world and we're not going to take anything of a material nature out of this world either. All we've ever done is just used what God gives to us or puts in our hands. We're stewards and we'll have to answer to Him. But I failed there.

Now lest you may misunderstand, let me insert this here. If you're in the business world, and you're there because that's where God wants you, and you have perfect peace in your heart, God will honor you just as much in the business world as He will honor me in the pulpit. When God has a call on your life for a certain ministry, you can't buy Him off by offering Him money as a substitute.

Trying to substitute money for a life I again lost my happiness and joy in what I was doing. I really tried my best to serve God at home with my family. I was superintendent of a Sunday school with an attendance between 650 and 700. I worked long hours in my business and began pouring thousands of dollars into the church treasury. I would go out trying to help preachers in their meetings, but somehow I couldn't find that deep settled peace that I needed. The reason was that God wanted me in the evangelistic field. I'd told Him I'd go anywhere He wanted me to go and then, I'd decided I could serve Him better at home and pour money into the church treasury.

That's when I lost my health. My friends pled with me. My pastor spoke to me. My business associates told me I never could keep up the pace I was going. My wife wept over me, pleading for me to please take more time to rest. But I'd keep saying, "I'll never break down; I'm a mountain man." I went into and came out of the service of my country with a perfect physical record. I'd always had a good, strong, healthy body. But you know, it wasn't the hard work that caused the break. It was the fact that I just didn't have that deep settled peace that I'd enjoyed so richly through those years, living in the center of His will. Anyhow, whatever the cause, the thing I thought couldn't happen happened.

I'll never forget that morning! I awakened from my sleep and I was experiencing real trouble in my chest in the area of my heart. It was palpitating heavily and as I got out of bed I found I'd become so very weak that I could scarcely stand on my feet. I was finally able to get dressed and go down to the kitchen. I was praying. It would soon be time to leave for Sunday school and I didn't know what was happening to me. I went outside and walked in

47

the backyard a few minutes, thinking this will surely pass soon.

I did make it to the church that morning and succeeded in getting through my duties as superintendent. But before I was through I could count every heartbeat through my coat. My heart was really laboring. I tried to make it back to our cottage on the hill, but I didn't make it. I fell by the side of the road with a violent heart attack.

My friends picked up my unconcious body, carried me into my home and immediately called the doctor. When he arrived, seeing my condition, he quickly summoned further help. From noon on Sunday until Monday morning those doctors never left my bedside. Those men were dear, close friends and how faithfully they worked to sustain life in my body.

My precious wife and children were praying during those long hours when it seemed every breath would be my last. My son, Bill, was only a little lad of about eleven. He often tells of how he cried for God to please spare his daddy through those anxious moments of waiting. I knew nothing of those agonizing hours for my family.

Finally, I came back to consciousness and looked up into the face of my doctor. His face was strained. When he saw I was conscious he said, "We've really had a bad time with you, Will. I thought you weren't coming back, but we couldn't give you up."

The reason I came back was that my mother had registered a prayer in heaven. In the meantime, she'd gone to be with the Lord. We didn't know she was dying, but the last word she spoke to me was this. Looking up into my face and leaning toward me she whispered, "Billy, someday you're going to preach." Her head fell back on the pillow and she was Home. She'd believed God and He'd promised, so that's why God allowed me to live—that I might tell this old, old story that's so dear to my heart.

There I was in that desperate condition. They discovered shortly that not only my heart, but my entire system had broken down. From that time on, one organ after another began to deteriorate. This continued for two years or more, even though I had the best attention as far as medical science was concerned. I thank God for all my doctors, for all of those engaged in alleviating suffering, doing what they can to bring back health and strength. But there just didn't seem to be any cure for my trouble. I kept going down and down, getting progressively worse until during the last stages of my illness I weighed less than a hundred pounds. My heart was so enlarged it was three times its normal size. It was constantly laboring to keep life in my body.

During one hospital stay they found I couldn't digest even the simplest kind of food. My lower bowel had been paralyzed for eighteen months. I was going blind. I had tried everything medical science had to offer. When they took drugs away from me, I tried osteopathy, then chiropractors. I got relief but no healing.

Finally, in that desperate state, I was again sent to still another hospital in the Pittsburgh area for a long period of diagnosis. My church believed that the Lord healed people, but only through doctors. They had taught us the day of miracles was past and when the doctors were through with you, God was through with you, too. All you could look for was the undertaker. So I had my confidence entirely in doctors.

On this occasion, they had the finest specialists in the country diagnose my case. They even had some visiting specialists from abroad come in to see me as I spent those many weeks in that hospital. I hoped and trusted they would find a way to bring back my health. Oh, how I longed to get well, to take my place in the world again! I wanted to serve God and take care of my family.

Finally, the evening came for my diagnosis. The doctors arrived at my bedside to give me their answer based on these extensive tests. I was hoping and praying they'd have a good report. I looked up as my doctor approached my bed. One look at his face and I had my answer. He was a very dear friend, and as he stood there and looked down at me for some moments before speaking, I saw a tear and then several start to trickle down his cheeks.

I know people tell you that doctors are hardhearted and some of them may be. They have to control their emotions to be able to minister as they do, but I had a very tenderhearted doctor, a very fine, kind and compassionate friend. He brushed the tears away with his hand and when he spoke, calling me by name, he said, "Will, do you really want to know the truth about yourself?"

I studied his face for a moment and said, "Well, Doc, it certainly wouldn't help to tell me an untruth. You know my responsibilities and so I'd sure like to know the truth."

The doctor said, "First of all, we don't know how you stay alive. Medically speaking, you should be dead and buried. Everybody who has examined you is puzzled at how you've lived this long. We do not know what is keeping you alive. We've done everything we can and you don't respond. You just keep going down and with that heart of yours in the condition it's in, plus all of these other added complications, it's just nothing short of amazing that you've continued to survive. We have no remedy for you. We're sorry, but we just do not have a cure."

He was truly a brokenhearted man. He started to leave and then turning again he said, "By the way, have you made a will?"

I replied, "No Doctor, I haven't. I'm sorry, but I've neglected to do that. I was counting on getting well. Are you sure there's no hope, nothing else they can do for me? Something new they can try?"

Doc just stood there slowly shaking his head. Then he said, "I'll call your lawyer and you can take care of that matter and then the best we can do for you is to relieve your suffering. We've decided to send you south with someone to take care of you. We believe you'll live longer in a warmer climate than you will here. We're going to help you all we can, but Will, we have absolutely no cure for your trouble."

The lawyer came and wrote my last will and testament. I reached out a trembling hand to sign away, with one stroke of the pen, everything that I'd struggled for. When I saw my signature, something happened in me, something I've been grateful for ever since. The love of things was lifted out of my heart and life. From that time on, I never again loved things—people and God, yes, but not things. Whatever God now puts in my hands, I recognize as His. I want to serve Him as a good steward, to live for Him. I want everything I do to glorify God, for I owe everything to Him.

That night in the hospital, I wept myself into a troubled sleep. I reminded myself I could've done what my mother had wanted and had dedicated me to do, but now it was too late.

A little later they sent me south. I had a splendid companion to travel with me. He was a Catholic by faith, but a wonderful friend and a fine practical nurse. We traveled by boat from Baltimore down to the Miami, Florida area. The rooms he secured were very comfortable and the climate was marvelous. But when you've left everything that's dear to your heart, and your body's wracked day and night with pain, it takes more than Florida sunshine and tropical breezes to cheer you up.

It seemed like God had forsaken me. The face of my Lord I could not find and I was a greatly troubled man. I felt worse than I did at home where at least my family could come to visit and pray with me.

Feeling so badly, I guess I began to give my nurse a good deal of trouble. Jimmy Carroll was his name. On one occasion he said, "I think if you'll look at this newspaper it might relieve your mind for a few minutes."

I could see the headlines all right. I could see the print momentarily, but usually when I'd start to read the pain became so unbearable I had to lay it aside. They'd told me that if I lived any length of time I'd become totally blind because the nerves to my eyes were also dying, as were all the other organs of my body. As they described it, the whole sympathetic nervous system was rapidly deteriorating. I also had a catarrhal condition beyond my power to describe. Since there was no saliva produced in my mouth, the gums decayed away and my teeth stuck out of a naked jaw bone.

But God, that day, had a message for me in that newspaper. I took the paper Jimmy handed me and the first thing I saw in bold black type was this announcement on the church page:

OLD-TIME REVIVAL — 33RD STREET AND 5TH AVENUE

Those meetings were being held in the large tabernacle auditorium of the Christian and Missionary Alliance in Miami, Florida. I didn't even see who was preaching. I didn't need to. The words, Old-Time Revival, struck a responsive chord in my lonely heart. Immediately I wanted to go there and this was contrary to all my desires up to this time. I wasn't even supposed to have company. I was to be kept quiet. This had been no problem as I was in such a miserable state I didn't want company anyhow. But, hear now, I did want to be taken to that revival.

I told my nurse, "When I've been in trouble before God has met me in a revival meeting. Of course, I've never been in a condition like I am now, but I'd like you to take me just once to that meeting."

He looked at me and replied, "Now, Will, you're asking an impossible thing. You know the orders. You're to be kept quiet. If I took you over in that crowd you'd probably get excited and just as likely slip out into eternity and I'd get the blame for it."

I said, "No, Nurse, you write anything you want to write, and I'll sign it, absolving you of all blame because I must be taken there." Somehow I knew I must attend. And how I thank my God that He implanted that desire in my heart. I hadn't given my doctors up; they'd given me up. Now God was ready to answer my mother's prayer.

My nurse, Jimmy, was still not sure he should listen to my pleadings. Again he reminded me I'd probably get excited and die on his hands if he listened to me.

Well, his hesitancy was getting me worked up too and I said, "If you don't take me, I'll just get excited here then!"

And as I began to get further agitated, he hurriedly said, "All right! All right! Don't get any more worked up here either. I'll take you this once—I can't resist your pleading—but only if you'll promise, that if it gets too much for you, in any way—I mean, like getting excited or emotionally involved—you'll then let me bring you right back here."

Jimmy took me to that service and it was the first time I'd ever been in a Christian and Missionary Alliance meeting. I didn't know anything about that denomination. They were holding a city-wide crusade in a tabernacle-type building, with yellow pine benches and sawdust floors. It seated about 2,500 people, and the Lord was blessing.

My nurse found a place for me near the rear of the auditorium. He propped me up with cushions and made me as comfortable as he could. In the moments that followed, I heard for the first time in a long time the old gospel story coming from that evangelist. My heart was touched as I saw people moved by the Spirit of God. Slowly a little light began to break into my darkened soul.

Then that preacher spoiled everything for me. He looked back my way, but I know he didn't see me for I was reclining. He said, "If there's somebody here tonight sick unto death and you cannot keep your health, if you'll yield your life to God and trust Him, He will heal your body the same as He saved your soul. For it doesn't take one ounce more faith to heal you than it did to save you. Jesus said to the palsied man, 'Whether is it easier to say to the sick of the palsy, Thy sins be forgiven thee; or to say, Arise, and take up thy bed, and walk?' (Mark 2:9). Belief in His resurrection power makes one miracle just as easy as the other."

Now I was forty-four years of age at the time and had never heard words like this from a pulpit in all my life and it shocked me! And you know, the old enemy got busy right away. He whispered, "You've gotten in with the wrong crowd. These folks are fanatics. They believe the Lord still heals the body. You'd better get out of here." And then he suggested to my mind that since I was very close to death, if I had to die, I'd better die orthodox. So I had my nurse get me out of there as quickly as possible.

As we were leaving I noted some Scripture banners with foot-high letters hanging on the walls and for which I thank God. Those verses became fastened on my mind. When we got back to our rooms I asked Jimmy to get my mother's Bible and see if those verses were in her Bible. I wanted him to read them to me.

He said, "Will, I've never had a Bible in my hands at any time in my life, but I'll try to help you." He had a rather bad time finding them, but with my help telling him where to look, he finally was able to read these words: "Jesus Christ the same yesterday, and today and forever" (Hebrews 13:8); "Who forgiveth all thine iniquities, who healeth all thy diseases" (Psalms 103:3), referring to our dear Lord. The third Scripture was Matthew 8:17: "Himself took our infirmities and bare our sicknesses."

When Jimmy had finished reading, the Lord spoke to my heart so sweetly saying, "Now that you've found these verses to be so and in your mother's Bible, will you trust Me?"

We began to study the Word of God. That is, my friend began to read the Word of God to me. He read it by the hour. I was determined to find out when God had quit this business of healing folks. I know the Lord helped Jimmy in his selections of portions to read, because it seemed practically every time he'd open that Book and begin to read, somebody was getting healed.

One day he stopped reading, looked me right in the eye and said, "You know, Will, if you'd believe what I'm reading I think the Lord would heal you."

I tried to talk myself out of it by replying, "You see, Jimmy, healing's not for our day. It's not for our time. The day of miracles is past."

His answer shook me a bit. "I don't know anything about this not being our day or time business, but I believe this is God's Word and if you'd do what He tells you, I believe He'd answer prayer and heal you, too." He had more faith than I did.

Finally, I was convinced that we ought to go back to that church where I'd heard this new truth, and now Jimmy was willing to take me. God had been dealing with his heart through all that Bible reading, and it says, "The entrance of thy words giveth light" (Psalm 119:130).

My nurse began to take me to the morning meetings where they read the Word of God and expounded it simply. Then they prayed for us. I got real help and encouragement from these sessions. The fourth morning I was there was the miracle morning. The night before I had a desperate struggle. It seemed my life would surely terminate before dawn. I was so weary, tired and helpless, so very sick and weak. I said, "Jimmy, I just can't make it to the service this time."

Then he became the aggressor. He looked at me and said, "Oh, yes, I think we can make it and really you'll be a lot better off in church than staying here."

Well, he persuaded me. He told me he'd take good care of me and finally we headed for the meeting place. This time he took me right down to the front. I believe I could go to the exact spot because that became a very special place to me that morning.

While I was waiting for the service to open, a gentleman came to where I was reclining, put his hand on my shoulder and spoke to me. I'd never seen him before but he said, "I don't know why I felt led to come to you but I'm in trouble."

I looked at him and said, "Well, if it will help you any, friend, if you'll notice, I'm in trouble too." You know, they say, trouble likes company.

"You don't understand," he said. "My wife's paralyzed. We have four little children. The doctors have given her up. I've spent all of my money. We heard that folks over here have been getting healed in these meetings, so I brought her today to these services. I came over to ask that you'd stand with me in prayer, that the Lord would spare my wife, heal her." Tears welled in his eyes, rolled down his cheeks.

I looked up and said to him, "You don't seem to understand the fact that I'm a dying man myself."

"Yes," he said, "I think I do. That's why you ought to know how to pray."

May I add here, prayer is not just saying a lot of words for folks to listen to. Prayer is a heart cry to a holy God, who hears and answers when we're sincere about it. So I said, "Well sir, I'll pray the best I can." And I meant it.

They called for prayer. I bowed my head and momentarily forgetting my own troubles and problems and sickness, I poured my heart out to God, as best I knew how, asking that He might please touch and heal my neighbor's wife.

And as I prayed for another, my wonderful heavenly Father gave me a marvelous revelation of Jesus my Savior, who not only took my sins but who also bore my sicknesses on Calvary. Thus Matthew 8:17 became a living reality to me through a divine revelation. I was so ignorant of this truth as I've already indicated. I'd never heard it or had it preached to me. I had always thought any such teaching was fanaticism. Now my wonderful Lord revealed to my heart that He had not only died for my sins but had also been beaten with many stripes that my broken body might be made whole.

Suddenly, something began to happen in my own body. I could sense it. I could feel the life of

God coursing through me. It began at the top of my head; and as this glorious sensation moved down through my body, as it reached the area of my heart, the load of so many weary months that weighed like lead, was suddenly gone. That old pump became as quiet and normal and peaceful as it had been when I was a young man. Then, right on down through the entire length of my body it continued. It was like warm oil flowing through me, flushing out all the ills of those long, weary months. Yes, the life of the Lord Jesus Christ, a transfusion of His divine life, flowed through every nerve center and fiber of my body.

You ask, "Could you feel it?'"

Yes, very definitely.

People ask, "Is it scriptural?"

Oh, yes! The woman who had the issue of blood for twelve years, felt in her body that she was healed when she touched the hem of Jesus' garment. In the same way, God knew He had to let me feel because I was so ignorant. I didn't know anything about these truths. I can trust Him now without feeling, but that morning I could feel the power and presence of God and when the prayer was finished, I was on my feet immediately. All fear was gone and I told the people assembled, "God has healed me." Up until this time I could only stand on my feet momentarily. My heart had become so weak that even to sit up for a few minutes would cause me to topple over unconscious. That old pump had been just too far gone to pump the blood to my head.

As I gave my testimony, I said, "Dear ones, I came into this place a dying business man. Something wonderful has happened to me. Praise God, I know I'm going to live." I walked down to the altar and two gentlemen came and touched my forehead with oil and committed me to the Lord, praying that the mighty work that God had wrought in my body that morning would continue through all my life.

God came down mightily on that service. There were about 1,000 people present. This wasn't done in a corner. I meet folks in my travels throughout the U.S. and Canada who were in that meeting and can also testify to the truth of my story. They've told me, "Brother Weston, we'll never forget that meeting. Our lives were changed by what happened there that day."

Well, praise the Lord, I went out of that service a new man. I was just as skinny as ever since I weighed less than a hundred pounds with my clothes and overcoat added. But I had life flowing; and also, I must add, my nurse friend, Jimmy, in that service, opened his heart and received the Lord Jesus Christ as his Savior, too.

We went back to the apartment where we'd been staying. I took one look at all that medication and especially, that predigested food and it almost made me ill again to look at it. I pitched the whole bit and we headed for the nearest restaurant. I was so hungry! Oh, how wonderful, just to have an appetite! You know, I've discovered it's far better to have a good appetite and no food than to have lots of food and no appetite. Amen!

Seated at the table in that restaurant we were soon approached by a little waitress. She looked at me and waited on me first. I guess she figured a fellow who looked like that needed immediate attention. The first thing that caught my eye on the menu was beefsteak and mashed potatoes. Oh my! Before I'd become ill I was a meat-and-potatoes man, so I pointed to that entree on the menu.

Smiling, she said, "You shall have it, Sir, with all the trimmings."

She then took Jimmy's order and departed into the kitchen. She soon reappeared and set that lovely dinner down in front of me. And right then, I suddenly had a visitor. Yes, the old devil put in an appearance. He whispered in my left ear, "Go ahead. Eat it, all of it. You know the doctors have warned you about attempting to eat anything that hasn't been predigested. Go ahead and in about two hours the nearest undertaking establishment will be preparing your body to ship back north." A comforting old rascal, to be sure.

Well, I knew that what he was saying was true. My doctors had repeatedly warned me that such food would decay in my stomach and the resulting liquids and gas would crowd my weakened heart and I'd be gone. But hallelujah! I also had another guest and He was immediately on the scene and whispered in my right ear—you see, God's always on the right side—"Listen, Son, what the enemy and your doctors told you was true yesterday, but today I took your infirmities and bore your sicknesses and with my stripes YOU ARE HEALED!"

Praise God! With that word echoing and reechoing in my heart I almost had camp meeting in that restaurant. I quietly bowed my head, thanked my heavenly Father and my wonderful Lord for my new divine life. Then I asked Him to especially bless this first real meal I'd had in years. Saying "Amen," I raised my head, smiled at Jimmy, who hadn't been tuned in on this very private conversation, and proceeded to eat and enjoy every bite on that plate.

And believe it. Everything was perfect. No indigestion. No problems at all. And from that time every organ of my body has functioned perfectly. My eyes could see, and even past eighty years of age I can still read without the aid of glasses. My gums grew back in my mouth. My entire body had been completely renewed by His power divine.

When we left the restaurant that day Jimmy hurried me to a telegraph office, where I sent the following wire: "Darling, bring the children. Come down. The Lord has healed me."

When my wife received that message—and remember, she was just as ignorant as I had been about this healing message—she threw herself across the bed and began to sob her heart out. She thought, "Dear Lord, he went away with a dying body and now he's lost his mind." My daughter, Bea, told me this later. I guess Mother was ashamed to tell me.

My wife brought the children and by the time they arrived in Miami, God had so rebuilt me that I could take my youngest son, Bob, off the platform of that train and lift him right up into the air. Mother said when she saw Bob going into the air a mountain lifted off of her soul, and she knew He had given her a new husband.

A little later in a very private session with the Lord, He said to me, "Now, can I have that life I've given back to you, that your mother dedicated to me so many years ago? May I have what's left of it?"

By that time, friends, I was through fighting God. It costs too much. So, broken of heart, I answered, "Lord, you know how sorry I am for all the failures. What's left of this life of mine is yours completely." Remember, I was forty-four.

God took me at my word, filled me with His Holy Spirit, put such a love in my heart for a lost world, that I could hardly wait to begin my ministry. I closed my business affairs and began my new life's work as an evangelist in the same tabernacle where God had touched me. I was healed February 7, 1926 and started my first campaign there on July 4 of that same year. You see, I didn't know that you couldn't have a revival crusade in the summertime down in Florida. Isn't it marvelous how God can work when you just have simple faith and trust Him?

In that first meeting I was only to give my testimony a few nights, but God broke through and it was five weeks before that meeting closed. I know of four men that are preaching the gospel who gave their hearts to Christ in that campaign. From that day to this, I've been traveling throughout the United States and Canada. The Lord completely rebuilt my body to what you see here tonight. I stand here weighing between 197 and 200 pounds. I've passed my eighty-first birthday and I've not missed a service in over thirty-six years. I have been able to conduct over 600 crusades for Christ.

God has so richly blessed. He's saved my entire family. He's supplied our every need. We've never lacked any good thing from the day we said the big eternal "yes" to the Lord. He's restored the years that the cankerworm had eaten. My deepest desire is to continue to tell the old, old story of redeeming love as long as Jesus spares me or until He comes. Isn't He a wonderful Savior?

Each time I finish my testimony, I feel that the half has never yet been told. But hear this, what the Lord has done for this poor man and his family, He will do for anyone who will trust Him. He is no respecter of persons. I'm sure there are those of you who are hearing this who have failed God in some area of your life. You've been discouraged, disheartened, maybe even depressed or oppressed by the enemy of your soul. Dear ones, hear this: My heavenly Father stands ready to meet you. He wants to solve those problems, untangle those snarled threads of your life, and give to you new life in Jesus Christ, His Son.

CHAPTER FOUR

Dad's Ministry

As a part of his Evangelistic Crusades, Dad also had daily morning services, Monday through Friday. These Victory Hour Sessions were truly unique Bible studies. As his son, I felt he was a master in presenting the most workable methods in practical righteousness. In fact, many of the pastors felt these one hour morning meetings were the top drawer services of the crusade. As one preacher put it, "I learned how to truly live the victorious life during Brother Weston's Victory Hour Meetings in my church."

At the conclusion of one such session, a dear old Georgian lady approached my father and expressed her appreciation in a most effusive manner. "Oh, Dawkta Weston, Ah have been so thrilled, just simply thrilled, by your Spirit-filled ministry this mawning. Ah jus feel you surely have It!"

Dad smiled, but politely replied, "No, dear friend, I do not have It."

A little nonplussed, she said, "Oh, Dawkta Weston, then we must pray that you get It."

Still smiling and still very gracious, Dad replied, "Dear lady, I don't want It."

She gasped, hand to her mouth, in real consternation. Before she could answer, Dad broke in with, "I'm sure you are referring to the Holy Spirit, but, my dear, never refer to the Holy Spirit as an IT. He is just as much a part of the Godhead as God the Father and God the Son. He came to do the office work of the first two—to lift up Jesus, to convict mankind of the necessity of repentance, confession and the acceptance of the Lord Jesus Christ as their Savior and Lord. So, I feel we're taking undue liberties when we refer to the third Person of the Trinity using the neuter pronoun, It."

Dad had no doctorates. He never received any earthly degrees. So this lovely southern lady was being ultracomplimentary when she called him "Dr. Weston." On second thought though, I reckon Dad could've been a doctor because he cured a ham one time. As his son, I've never attained that status or honor either. I've always wanted to be a doctor, but just never had the patients. Tsk!

Miracles were a part of Dad's life. His own miraculous healing was a definite confirmation of God's power to resurrect life out of death, a true twentieth century miracle. As a result, God gave him a special gift of faith in praying for others. Perhaps it would be better terminology to say our heavenly Father endowed him with the gift of healing.

The Scriptures show that the early disciples were so endowed by the Master. "And when He had called unto Him His twelve disciples, He gave them power against unclean spirits, to cast them out, and to heal all manner of sickness and all manner of disease" (Matthew 10:1). And it is recorded in John that "Greater works than these shall ye do; because I go unto my Father" (John 14:12). Hebrews 13:8 is most certainly still in the Book: "Jesus Christ the same yesterday, and today, and forever."

Anyway, God gave this marvelous gift to Dad on so very many occasions. No fanaticism; just a simple childlike faith, putting the Scriptures given by our Lord into practice.

> And Jesus answering saith unto them. Have faith in God. For verily I say unto you, That whosoever shall say unto this mountain, Be thou removed, and be thou cast into the sea; and shall not doubt in his heart, but shall believe that those things which he saith shall come to pass; he shall have whatsoever he saith. Therefore I say unto you, What things soever ye desire, when ye pray, believe that ye receive them, and ye shall have them. (Mark 11:22-24)

In our ten years together as a father-and-son team, I personally witnessed many "mountains" removed from lives. The following stories are true. I can verify them. I was there.

It was in Richmond, Virginia, that I witnessed one of the most amazing, miraculous answers to prayer. We were headed south for another series of evangelistic meetings. Our first stop was a one-night stand in Richmond.

Carried into the meeting that evening was Hamilton P. Rankin, a man dying of sarcoma cancer of the face. He was just released from one of the major cancer-research hospitals on the east coast, as a hopeless, incurable case. He came that night to receive Christ as his Savior and Lord. You see, you can get to heaven with a sick body, but you can't enter those sinless portals with a sick soul.

Upon seeing this man, I agreed with the doctors; I wouldn't have given a plugged nickel for his chances to survive even another day. But that's the human outlook, not God's! As I looked, I thought, *What an emaciated piece of rotten flesh*. He was just skin and bones, with one side of his face the color of raw liver. The hair on his head was white as snow. That dreaded cancer had eaten up through the roof of his mouth and was now nearing his brain. He was daily sedated with heavy dosages of drugs to alleviate the unbearable pain.

Then, prayer was offered, registered in heaven and concluded with that word, " Amen"—so be it. Dad usually said to the one being prayed for, "Now beloved, that's settled. Praise the Lord!" And it was, but the visible answer was delayed more than a year.

My father and I were in New York City, at the Simpson Tabernacle, conducting a week of special meetings. After a Sunday morning service we were walking up one of the aisles to meet our hosts with whom we were to have Sunday dinner when I heard, "Hi! Brother Bill. Hello, Daddy Weston." Quite frankly, I didn't know the man who had spoken and my father's reply indicated he didn't either. Dad said, "We've evidently met you somewhere before, but where I truly am at a loss to say."

"Of course you wouldn't remember me, Brother Weston," the man said. "When last you saw me I was just a shell of a man eaten up with cancer. I'm Hamilton Rankin, the man you anointed and prayed for during that one-night meeting in Richmond, Virginia. I'm now attending Nyack Bible School, Brother Weston, preparing for the ministry."

No wonder we didn't recognize him. There he was, such a rugged specimen of manhood—about 190 pounds, coal-black hair (it had been snow white when we saw him in Richmond) ruddy complexion—the picture of virility and robust health. To be sure, we rejoiced as we witnessed God's handiwork, His power manifested in such a miraculous, marvelous deliverance. PRAISE THE LORD!

The epilogue should be added here: H.P. Rankin was attending Nyack, his expenses paid by his death insurance benefits. He was the only man I've ever heard of who was going to school on his own death insurance monies. Before long, H.P. told us, he got convicted for what he was doing. He went to that insurance company's headquarters, was ushered into the president's office, told his story. The agent, convinced through the hospital's records and seeing H.P.'s condition firsthand, had presented Mrs. Rankin with the check. Since H.P. would obviously be dead very soon, the insurance man thought it would save a return trip to Richmond.

The president was visibly moved upon hearing H.P.'s testimony of God's delivering power and seeing the results firsthand. "What an amazing story!" he exclaimed. "And you are going to Bible school, preparing for the ministry?" Still shaking his head, he added, "Well, as I look at it, according to our records, Rankin, you're dead. Use the money as you are doing with our endorsement, and God bless you."

As great as this testimony may be, the greatest miracle ever wrought among men is the new birth. In one moment, God transforms a life from a hellbent sinner into one of His saints heading for the celestial city. That's a miracle like no other.

It happened in Ft. Lauderdale, Florida, during a big tent crusade. Into the service one evening stumbled, and I do mean stumbled, an old bum, a drunken wretch by the name of Daddy Fry. We'd heard of him. His reputation had preceded him. In fact, there were few in that area of the country that hadn't heard of this character. A rumrunner, he had been in the news often. To most, the mere mention of his name caused even decent folks to resort to some pretty undeniably descriptive language. We had heard things like, "He's scum!" and "A drunken filthy bum." The non-Christians were even more explicit, using terminology not usually included in Webster's tome of desirable words. But, there he was, big as life, in the tent.

An usher hurried to the platform. He had hastily scribbled the following note on the back of an offering envelope: "The drunk who just came in, and he's pretty soused, is Daddy Fry. He's a pretty unsavory bird. Shall we put him out?"

Upon reading this message, Dad replied, "Put him out? Never. I've heard too many of you townspeople praying to get him in that he might get saved."

The usher was a little abashed, but figured that answer made sense. Quickly he retraced his steps to convey Dad's message to those who had assumed the responsibility of handling the situation. Meaning, of course, Daddy Fry.

Meanwhile, my father quietly committed the problem to his heavenly Father, asking that divine intervention take over. In short order, Daddy Fry suddenly simmered down. He lost his bellicose, fire-in-the-eye demeanor, and became as calm and serene as any good Sunday-morning parishioner.

He listened to the sermon, and then, as the invitation hymn, "Just As I Am," was announced, he made this loud declaration: "I wanna go up there to that preacher. Gotta talk to the parson."

They brought him forward, a man on either side supporting his reeling torso. Finally, he was standing before an old-fashioned mourners' bench—an altar, to those not remembering such good, Methodist terminology. Gripping the bench with one hand, his eyes so bleary they looked like they were bleeding, he confronted my father.

A tent full of people watched, intrigued by what was happening. Some were even standing on seats to get a better look. The local folk couldn't believe their eyes. Daddy Fry, a penitent!

Dad took over that unique counseling session. He first tried to explain the plan of salvation. It was difficult, as that liquor-soaked brain couldn't comprehend. His eyes couldn't even focus.

"Wot?" he stammered, his words hard to come by. "Ya sa-sa-say, Gawd can fo-for-forgiiive meee? Ah, no, pre-preacher, na-na-not meee. Gaawd could n-e-v-e-r ffoorrgive mmeee. I've been too bad. Just ask any of theese peeooople here. They all know me." His bleary eyes sought out that crowd for confirmation.

"Dontcha?" he asked.

"After what I've been and done? Noooo. Oh no, Gawwwd couldn't ever for-forgive meee, neveer. Gawd couldn't pos-pos-possibly forgive or love me. No siree, not after what I've done. Why I've murdered." A sudden surge of remembering and remorse seemed to engulf him then. Sobbing, he repeated, "Oh, dear God, I, I, I ki-killed people."

Dad's voice quickly broke in, overriding further garbled statements of "I'm a murderer, yes I am; I've killed people." Feeling such admissions in his inebriated state inadvisable, Dad changed the course of the conversation by saying, "Daddy Fry, listen, listen to me. I don't care how bad you've been or what you've done. If you will just confess to God, He will forgive you—blot out your miserable past. Whether you believe it or not, God does love you and He proved it by letting His Son, the Lord Jesus Christ, die for you, too."

Then, as if suddenly inspired—and I'm sure he was—my father said, "Daddy Fry, listen. If God would sober you and cause you to become sick, deathly sick, when you drink that hellish stuff that's made you a drunkard, would you believe then that God loves you?"

Before he replied, I wish you could've witnessed what happened. His befuddled mind, disbelieving what he'd just heard, was mirrored in his face. You could almost hear the wheels turning in his mind. "Preacher, you've lost your marbles. Yer plumb off your rocker."

Then, as his bewildered thoughts suddenly came into focus, he doubled over with raucous laughter. And then again, just as quickly, he became sober and serious. Raising his hand, index finger pointed toward that crazy preacher, he sputtered, "Dear Gawd, parson, do you know what you just said? Listen. Me, who haint drawed a sober breath in fourteen years, yer tellin' me, that I can't go outa this place, right now, and lap up a quart of whiskey, in one setting? Well now, look here"—and he cussed—"I'd know, of course, I'd shor as [cuss word] would know God loved me."

Reader friend, whether you choose to believe this account or not, it happened. Several pastors and laymen gathered around that old drunk, and with a tent full of people looking on, my father prayed. He asked for the Almighty to prove His love by delivering Daddy Fry from his lifetime habit, to make him deathly sick at the first mouthful he'd attempt to drink.

What a precious Savior we have! Deity bent low to hear that petition. The very powers in Heaven above were moved. The Father and Son, in session together, decided to send an immediate reply. That old man left the tent, still drunk. He was assisted to his home, where the men left him lying on his bed, still in a drunken stupor.

He evidently fell asleep for a time. Awaking about three in the morning, he reached for his ever-present bottle of booze. At 3:15 a.m., the phone rang in the place where we were staying. Believe me, calls at that hour alert an entire household. Dad was the first to the phone. He lifted the receiver and got this message: "Preacher, God loves me! Come right away. Oh dear God, please help me. I'm so sick! Tried to drink and I can't keep a drop down."

Praise the Lord! What a tremendous miracle. Daddy Fry was completely delivered. Our wonderful heavenly Father had so marvelously answered prayer! He took that hellish drug right out of Daddy Fry's bloodstream. Later on, he led his two sons to Christ. Kneeling between them, arms hugging their burly shoulders—they were such big bruisers—he told them, "Boys, Jesus will save you. Yes, He will. He will forgive you. You know He can and will after the way He's met your old Dad." And both sons, seeing the miracle of the new birth, the transformation in their father, invited Christ to come in and become their Savior, too.

A few days later one of the news reporters checking with the sergeant at the desk in city jail was told, "We don't have any news. Haven't you heard? There's nobody in the cells here. Daddy Fry's got religion and he's getting all the old drunks and sinners converted. I think it would be a good idea to turn this place over to that Yankee evangelist and let him hold his meetings here instead of in that big tent."

The reporter spread that news, posthaste, across the front page: "Daddy Fry has hit the sawdust trail. Sgt. at city jail suggests turning same over to tent preacher for series of meetings." What an advertisement for the tent crusade! We couldn't have purchased that advertising space, I reckon, for under $1,000.

How did it impact that southern city? Well, when Daddy Fry was baptized in the Atlantic Ocean at 6 A.M., nearly 2,000 people stood on the beach to watch. And believe it, emotions ran high as they watched Daddy Fry, arms extended upwards, walk out into the water, tears streaming down his old weather-beaten face. But the glow of heaven was there too, and he was saying over and over again, "Dear Jesus, I'm not worthy, but thank you, thank you. Thank you for loving and saving me."

I repeat: There's no greater miracle than the new birth, a life changed, transformed in a moment of time. What a wonderful Savior we have; one who is interested in the minutest details of our lives. The songwriter says it so well, "The Savior can solve every problem, the tangles of life can undo. There's nothing too hard for Jesus, there's nothing that He cannot do."

Dad wrote a proverb that I'd like to insert here: "If you'll pray as much to keep out of trouble, as you do to get out of trouble, you won't get into trouble." Try it, because if really practiced, it works.

Dad's ministry appealed to all ages. It was the delight of his heart when little children were responsive to his messages. He loved them so dearly. He felt when they would come for prayer that his heavenly Father was surely smiling because this was according to His Word. Jesus encouraged children to come. He said, "Suffer the little children to come unto me, and forbid them not: for of such is the kingdom of God" (Mark 10:14) and "Except ye be converted and become as little children, ye shall not enter into the kingdom of heaven" (Matthew 18:3).

Dad loved to relate this story about a little four-year-old girl, who came weeping to the altar. Feeling she might be ill, Dad hurried to where she was kneeling. As big folks are so very prone to do, he misjudged her reason for coming by asking, "Honey, are you sick?" Before he could add a further word, her reply changed the whole atmosphere, his whole trend of thinking.

With surprise in her voice and big blue eyes, she said, "Oh no, Brother Weston, I'm not sick. I'm just such a big old sinner."

To which, Dad so wisely replied, "Well, darling, Jesus died for big old sinners just like you." Then, he prayed with her as she so sweetly opened her heart and received the Savior.

I initiated Dad into the booster club program. How his eyes would sparkle when I'd have those children who could remember something he'd preached about in his message the previous evening come to the platform and whisper what it was in his ear. Some would tell him several things, even give a whole outline.

Maybe I'd better explain just what that program is all about. Using the thought, "A little child shall lead them," I organize two teams of youngsters, usually in the five-to-twelve-years-of-age span. A real competitive spirit is generated as they then try to gain points for their team through a daily personalized invitation system. Each night they are present they count 25 points for their team. The object is to add to their team's roster by inviting their little school chums and friends to participate, thus mushrooming their attendance figures. Moms and Dads count 100 points every night they are present. Grandparents are worth 150 points at every service they attend. First-timers among school friends, neighbors, kinfolk and others are worth 100 points.

Then, the point scale rises with 500 points for school teachers; 1,000 for principals, firemen, police and nurses; 1,500 points for doctors, lawyers, fire and police chiefs; 2,000 for judges, city councilmen, aldermen, and I've added bankers to this grouping just to keep up their interest.

Points then go way up: 5,000 points for mayors; 7,500 for State Representatives; and if they could get the governor to come, I would tell them they'd automatically win. To maintain discipline, if they wiggled or whispered too much, they would lose points. And, if they dared to pinch it would really penalize their team.

One thing I know: it works. I've seen churches filled to capacity as these precious young ones became involved in the family life crusades. You see, it's difficult to say "no" to an invitation from a child. We've had many mayors, even of major cities, police, firemen and all of the others just mentioned, represented in the meetings. Twenty-two firemen came with a little girl one night. She'd gone to the station house to invite them and she was as proud as punch as she introduced them and thus gained 22,000 points for her team.

The police chief of Syracuse came on a little tyke's invitation. As I recall, it was at a drive-in restaurant. Recognizing the chief's cruiser parked nearby, that little fellow was out of that car and over asking, "Are you the police chief?"

"Yes, I am, Son."

"Well sir, would you please come as my guest to the meetings at our church and help my team win because you're worth 1,500 points, sir?"

Of course, the chief came. The Syracuse newspaper carried the story the next day on the editorial page, two columns wide: "Police Chief goes to church with little boy."

A former governor in North Carolina received thirty-two phone calls. He couldn't attend due to special legislative sessions. However, he wrote a letter to one little chap who had called inviting him to come. I'd vote every time for a man like that. He was graciousness personified. You can trust a fellow that has a heart big enough to love and take time to listen to children.

President Carter has also received telephone calls and letters. I really didn't have the president listed on the point chart so I figured those youngsters reckoned if they could get our Commander-in-Chief, his total of points wouldn't be peanuts. Anyhow, I've added this as background for the story of Dad's first introduction to our booster club program.

I flew in from St. Louis, Missouri, where I directed Youth For Christ for forty-five years, to be with Dad in this particular meeting on the East Coast. One of the men of that congregation had divorced his wife, who was an alcoholic. He was fearful that she might seriously hurt their children during one of her drunken stupors.

One evening, his children, who had become involved in our booster club, invited their mother to come to the services. They still loved her, even though their little lives were so very much tied into this whole traumatic experience. As children, they were able to reach their mother's heart and she came to the Wednesday evening meeting. Those youngsters were ecstatic! She was a bit under the influence, but she listened as Dad spoke that evening. Her husband, a very gracious man, welcomed her warmly. He was so happy she had consented to come. Through the years his efforts to get her involved in church-related activities had been stymied. She wanted nothing to do with that religious bit.

Thursday night she was back again. Why? Because her children insisted she be there. It was very obvious she had been drinking, but again she sat quietly, caused no disturbance and listened intently.

Friday evening God brought her back once more because that was the night Deity decided to step in and straighten out this mess that self, sin and Satan had designed to break up a home. That evening she came as a penitent, broken soul before the Lord, seeking His mercy. And the Lord Jesus Christ, through His Spirit, took up residency within her heart at her request. Forgiveness was granted. An inner peace invaded her soul and for good measure, God cleansed that drug and all desire for it right out of her bloodstream. What a transfusion and transformation! Praise the Lord! The immediate reaction: a family of five, clustered in one big embrace, were reunited. Our wonderful Lord smiled down on that beautiful scene. A home was restored. That Sunday they were remarried.

In subsequent trips together, Dad and I often chatted about that marvelous conversion experience. Years have passed and those faces have rather dimmed now, but I'll never forget that service. It's indelibly imprinted in the memory section of my mind, and I can pull it down, as it were, and so vividly recall that husband's face especially. He was as bald as a billiard ball. I reckon he thanked the Lord daily for eyebrows. I can see him now—his countenance radiating happiness, with a seeming halo atop his pate. Of course, it might have been the light bouncing back from a ceiling chandelier. The dark clouds of years were dispersed; the sun had at last broken through. In that moment, his marriage and home were restored and revitalized.

A dear pastor friend of mine, whose noggin also resembles heaven—no parting there—has so often chided me about making light of the balding. He told me of a chap, who becoming sparse on top, used to comb his hair across his head from ear to ear. When asked, "Doesn't it bother you now to comb your locks that way instead of straight back as you did before?"

"No," he replied. And then with second thoughts, added, "Well, yes, sometimes I guess it does bother me a mite when folks come up and whisper in my nose."

On another occasion, we had meetings with Rev. Jarvis Conley, at that time pastor of the West End Alliance Church in Williamsport, Pennsylvania. I recall this incident following a Thursday evening service. During my father's ministry, it was always a pattern of his to reserve that weeknight for a message exalting the Lord Jesus Christ as the Great Physician. Following that particular service we were invited to the home of one of the finest doctors within that city. He was a devoted Christian, and had in fact been one of the group of elders and laymen assisting around the altar during the prayer time. Many had responded to the invitation to come with their varied spiritual and physical needs and it was more than Dad and I could handle by ourselves.

In their home, this very gracious physician and his wife provided refreshments. Then after some moments of conversation he said, "Brother Weston, I know the Lord can and does heal these bodies of ours. In fact, I think you'll recall that I assisted one of the prayer groups ministering to those who came forward this evening. However, I must be honest and say I do take exception to one of your statements in your message this evening."

My father smiled and replied, "Well, Doc, I'm happy there's only one statement wherein we differ because I think it will be easy to resolve it quickly with the help of our Lord. What's the problem?"

The Doctor answered, "Brother Weston, you preach as though it's God's will to heal everyone and I personally can't accept that."

Dad quietly responded, "Beloved, will you kindly show me in the Scriptures where the Lord has changed His will for His children? And would you have me believe our God then is a respecter of persons, when I've always been taught that He isn't? I read in Acts 10:38 that the Lord Jesus Christ came to do the will of His Father and He healed them all. Then, on another occasion, when the disciples failed in their ministry, the Master rebuked them and then healed the sick one, proving that though man may fail because of weak faith, God's program and ministry remains intact, unfailing. Now, Doctor, to follow this further, do you have children?"

"Yes, I do, Brother Weston."

"Well then, have you, as a good, loving father ever wanted any of them to be sick, or desired that they at any time should be afflicted with some disease?" Before the doctor could reply, Dad continued. "I'm sure I already know your answer to those questions. Can you really believe then, that our heavenly Father's will for His children would be less compassionate than your will for your family?"

"Now, Doctor, let me ask you this question. How long have you been a medical doctor in this city?"

Our doctor friend replied, "Over fourteen years, Brother Weston."

"Did you, in all of that time, ever refuse service?" Dad asked. "I mean, have you ever neglected to administer aid to any patient that called? I guess what I really want to know is, did you ever say 'no' to any patient needing your services?"

That splendid physician revealed just a smidgen of pride when he answered, "Brother Weston, with God as my witness, and as a dedicated doctor who well remembers the oath I took when I entered this profession and became a physician, no, sir, never once have I denied my services to any patient. As you know, we get calls at all hours of the day and night, but I'm truly proud of my record in this regard. I've always gone, sir, and my dear wife can bear witness to that also."

His wife nodded assent.

What happened then, I think rather surprised them both. Dad quietly arose, crossed the room to where the doctor and his wife were seated on a couch, and, extending his hand said, "Doctor, may I congratulate you."

"Oh, Brother Weston, I didn't mean it that way. I wasn't in any way seeking or wanting any praise for what I think or consider is just a dedicated doctor's duty."

Dad reassured him by answering, "I understand that perfectly, dear friend, but no, hear me out. I just felt I must congratulate you because, by your own admission, your compassion for your patients, for those afflicted with some disease, exceeds the love and compassion of our heavenly Father."

Taken aback, the doctor got to his feet and stammered, "Oh, Brother Weston, what do you mean, I . . ."

To which my Father hurriedly countered, pouring oil on troubled waters. "My dear doctor friend, it's this way. You say no matter when they call, you always respond and try to minister to their varied ills, trying to help, to cure them. Right?"

"Yes."

"Well, doctor, if you'll recall the beginning of this conversation, your opening statement indicated you feel God wants some people to remain sick. Leastwise, I understood you to mean that, since you said I preach as though it's God's will to heal everyone and that you personally couldn't accept that. May I now ask this question? Since you are a Christian physician, wanting to do the will of God in your own personal life, when you go to visit your patients, how do you differentiate between those whom God wants to heal and those whom He, according to your thinking, wants to remain sick? I mean, doctor, how do you know which ones to prescribe medicine or pills to because, as a Christian doctor, you obviously can't work against God and try to cure those He's trying to keep sick, can you?"

That doctor's face was a picture to behold as my father continued to speak.

"You're a splendid physician and my dear brother in Christ. How deeply I admire your dedication, but

in spite of your skills and knowledge, I'm sure you'll
admit that though you want to, there are many of
your patients that you cannot help or cure. However,
your will doesn't change, doctor, but being human,
neither do you hold all the answers to life and death.
My Lord and Savior, on the other hand, does hold all
those answers, the keys, and believe it, His will never
alters nor changes."

That precious Christian doctor, smitten with
conviction, began to cry. With tears streaming
from his eyes, he fell on his knees and pleaded with
God. "Oh, dear Father in heaven, please forgive me
for even one moment thinking my compassion
could ever exceed yours. Lord Jesus, I'm so sorry for
that brash statement questioning your willingness
to provide for all of your creation's needs."

It was a beautiful prayer and at its conclusion,
that gracious gentleman arose to his feet and
walked over to where my father was now standing.
"Brother Weston," he said, "I am eternally indebted to you for these moments shared this evening. Thank you so very much for coming to our
home, for being my friend." The hand clasp and
further words of appreciation that followed, ce-
mented a friendship between that doctor and my
dad that lasted across the years.

No, everyone doesn't get healed. Why? Oh, how
I wish I could find someone that could answer that
question. But then again, not everyone gets saved
either, do they? The Word says, "Many are called,
but few are chosen"(Matthew 22:14). It also says,
"Enter ye in at the strait gate: for wide is the gate,
and broad is the way, that leadeth to destruction,
and many there be which go in thereat: Because

strait is the gate, and narrow is the way, which leadeth unto life, and few there be that find it" (7:13-14). Matthew further tells us of Jesus' teaching on this subject: "Many will say to me in that day, Lord, Lord, have we not prophesied in thy name? and in thy name have cast out devils? and in thy name done many wonderful works? And then will I profess unto them, I never knew you: depart from me, ye that work iniquity" (Matthew 7:22-23).

Yet the Bible declares, "And whosoever will, let him take the water of life freely" (Revelation 22:17). Why, oh why won't they come? Why do they choose death rather than life? Why do they choose to miss God and heaven and rather go to hell? Do I blame God? Never. It is not His will that is to be questioned. Man's will is the problem.

And, so it is with this healing message. There's no room for fanaticism here. Matthew 8:17 is still in the Book; it's still as valid for our day as it was when the Master trod this old sod–"Himself took our infirmities, and bare our sicknesses." Hebrews 13:8 is also still true: "Jesus Christ the same yesterday, and today and forever." And to be the same He must do the same works, and no one has been given His authorization to alter that statement. He also said, "[G]reater works than these shall he do; because I go unto my Father" (John 14:12). My old Dad took this stand on God's Word and I, his son, stand with him one hundred percent.

A beloved pastor friend of another denomination—and if you think you know which one it was, well, it was another one—also took exception to Dad's ministry on the Great Physician. In fact, this

particular group forbade this message being presented by their clergymen. To them it was radical
fanaticism, almost heresy and just could not be tol-
erated, let alone condoned. Divine healing was out.
It was not for our day. I can't recall that they had
consulted with the Almighty on the matter, and I
never did hear of any Scripture references given to
back their stand. Nor, to my knowledge, did they
ever indicate just when it was that Deity withdrew
such help from afflicted people. All I could find out
was that it just wasn't in the program authorized by
their organization. You see, they figured God had
provided doctors and hospitals and clinics to meet
twentieth century man's needs.

On that day, due to the trend the conversation
had taken, our pastor friend was a mite irritated.
He burst out, "Weston, if I believed like you do I'd
go out and empty the hospitals."

Dad just smiled and kept his cool. When he
spoke, his voice was quiet. "Beloved, you're a good
friend and a God-fearing, gospel-preaching, pas-
tor-evangelist. Do you believe it's God's will to save
everyone?"

He replied immediately, "Of course. He died for
all men and whosoever will may come. But how's
that related to healing? I think . . . ."

Dad broke in. "Well then, to follow your thinking, if I believed like you, and I most emphatically
do, why don't you go out and get them all saved?"

After a pause, he added, "I repeat, and I'll
stand on this statement forever, dear friend:
God's perfect will doesn't change. God's not at
fault here. In the Old Testament He was the
healer of His people. He brought the children of

Israel out of Egypt with silver and gold and not a sick one in all their company. In the New Testament Jesus came to do the will of His Father and He healed them all. No one did He turn away. Oh, no, my brother, neither you nor I nor anyone can alter God's will. I repeat, His work still declares that He's the same yesterday, today and forever and to be the same He still must do the same things today that He did in the yesterdays."

His pastor friend had no rebuttal.

To further challenge any who feel God's will has altered, Dad used to include the following: "I think you will agree with me that no parent, worthy of being a mom or dad, would ever go to any one of their children and say, 'Now look, you've been well a long spell. I believe it's about time you came down with the whooping cough, measles or chickenpox.' Your reply would certainly be, 'How very ridiculous!' Then, dear ones, how can we have the audacity to suggest that it is our heavenly Father's will for His children that are part of His family to be so afflicted?

"Sickness came as a curse upon the human race because of sin. The Lord Jesus Christ, when He died on the cross, dealt a death blow to sin and its resultant curse. We preach that man can be delivered from his sin, every sin, if he will repent, confess, believe and receive the Savior into his heart. If Jesus broke the curse, why, when, or where is it recorded that our heavenly Father altered His will with regard to physical needs? The answer is nowhere. We still have the prescription in James 5:14-15: 'Is any sick among you? Let him call for the elders of the church and let them pray over him, anointing him with oil in the name of the Lord; And the prayer of faith shall save the sick and the Lord shall raise him up; and if he have committed sins, they shall be forgiven him.' To be saved from sin we apply the Scriptures. To be healed, we also find our answers in the Word."

It was in a little city in Eastern Canada that the following miracle of divine grace and love took place. A Mrs. John Foster was carried into a morning "Victory Hour" service. She was suffering from tuberculosis of the bones, a dreadful disease that destroys the marrow within the bone. To multiply her problems she had fallen and broken her hip. Medicine inserted to alleviate suffering would simply flow on through, draining out at her knee.

That morning, with her body wracked with pain, she listened so very intently as my father exalted the Lord Jesus Christ as the Great Physician for those with physical needs. As he ministered the Word, a living, vibrant, mustard-seed faith sprang up within her heart. When the message ended, Mrs. Foster immediately requested prayer. The pastor and elders of that church gathered to join in faith in the administering of God's personal prescription for His sick children, as found in James 5:14. As Dad knelt he asked, "Beloved, do you believe God is able to meet your need and when do you expect Him to heal you?"

She replied instantly, "Oh, Brother Weston, I know He's not only able, but He's willing too, and I believe when you pray, I'm going to be completely healed."

The presence of the Lord was very real. He was there and those combined prayers ascended to the throne room of God. Mrs. Foster began to stir, attempting to arise from her prone position. Her husband, John, unaware of what was taking place in her body, quickly moved to assist, to keep her, as he thought, from falling to the floor. Not to be thwarted, however, in her efforts to get to her feet she said, "Get out of the way, dear. God has taken over my case. Oh, praise the Lord! Glory to God! Jesus has touched me and I'm healed! Oh, bless God! The Lord has healed me! Look! Oh, look, everybody, what God is doing!"

And, dear reader, before that audience, Mrs. Foster stood to her feet. Her restored hip held her weight. She paraded those aisles, tears of joy flowing down her cheeks, face aglow, voicing her praise, her gratitude, to her wonderful Savior and Lord. She was a witness to one and all that the glorious day of miracles is not past to those who will in simple childlike faith believe, accept and step out on the sure promise contained within that Book of Books. It is the living Word of an almighty, never-failing God.

The next day, she gave further evidence of the complete restoration of that hip, and her marvelous deliverance. She walked and ran across an acre of plowed ground to share with her neighbors about God's goodness to her and the Foster household.

God also has His hand in the everyday affairs and happenings of our lives. Romans 8:28 is for real. All things do work together for good. He does do things well. Dad and I discovered this while we were holding revival meetings at the Tabernacle in Ottawa, the capital city of Canada. My wife, Sally, was with us on this occasion and she and I were entertained in the home of our very dear friends, the Harold Beardsley family.

We had a good meeting. Many were revived and met the Lord for varied needs. The Ottawa Tabernacle had been packed that closing Sunday evening. In fact, the crowd overflowed out into the foyer of that big auditorium as Dad recounted the story of his life: "From Log Cabin to the Pulpit Via the Valley of the Shadow of Death."

Early the next morning, Sally and I said goodbye to our hosts, packed our suitcases into the car and headed for Uncle Walter J. Bauer's residence where Dad had been staying during those meetings. (Perhaps I should explain. The Bauers were not blood relatives, but the Weston clan thought of Uncle Walter and Aunt Gertrude as kinfolk because those dear ones had entertained the whole Weston household so very many times at their summer cottage at Norway Bay, Quebec.)

A light rain was falling as we traveled north on Bank Street that morning. The wooden, oil soaked, square blocks that made up the paving twixt the streetcar tracks had become as slick as a waiter's apron in the proverbial greasy-spoon restaurant. We had been forewarned by many of our Ottawa friends to drive carefully over those blocks during any wet weather, so we were proceeding cautiously. Leastwise, I thought we were.

At that particular moment, we were in the wake of a streetcar also heading north on that busy thoroughfare. Suddenly, it stopped. You guessed it. We didn't. The natural reaction was to hit the brakes and we found out firsthand just how slippery and treacherous those wooden blocks could be. We just kept sliding, skidding, straight toward the tender protruding from the rear of that streetcar. I spun the steering wheel, and the wheels turned all right but the car's direction never altered no matter how hard I tried. Unable to maneuver us off those blocks, we kept sliding straight ahead.

Sally and I had time to brace ourselves for the unavoidable impact we both could see was coming. WHAM! If we only could have actually taken that jolt with our bumper, the damage would have been negligible. But that tender was above and beyond the line of duty. Our dear old Chevy's grill grimaced, I'm certain, then winced, wrinkled and let go. The radiator also decided to do a hasty retreat back into the engine, which, as you can imagine, stubbornly resisted such an intrusion. Wotta chain reaction! Wotta mess!

Did you ever get that queasy feeling way down in your innards? Well, then you'll know our reaction as we clambered out of the car to survey the damage. We didn't hurt that stupid streetcar one iota. And no, I didn't stand there and say "Praise the Lord," either. Maybe I should've since we weren't hurt physically, but somehow or other it just never occurred to me at that moment to sing the Doxology. I was upset. All of our well-laid plans for an early departure for the good old U. S. A. and home had to be shelved. Why, oh, why did this have to happen?

Hurrying to a phone booth, I called Dad. God love him, he didn't get a bit upset. As always, he was so understanding and gracious, so solicitous about our welfare rather than concerned as to what had happened to the car. Then he said rather matter-of-factly, "Accidents will happen, Son, and I'm sure you didn't mean to run afoul of that vehicle. Now don't worry, we'll get it taken care of. I'm just so very thankful you and Sally are OK!"

What a Dad! He didn't at all bless that streetcar like I did.

Telephone calls were made. Friends quickly arranged for towing to a garage where we would be able to get immediate repairs done.

But again the question, why? Well, here's why: A mother traveling with her dying baby, via train from mid-Canada, near Winnipeg, had arrived in Ottawa late Sunday night after the meeting was ended. She had hoped to have the evangelist anoint and pray for her baby, but discovered he was already on his way to the States. But God, knowing about that mother's problem, that very sick baby and the faith that had prompted that long trip, had altered plans. He just sort of allowed me to tangle with that nice streetcar, so that we would be detained an extra day in Ottawa.

Finding the Bauer's telephone number, this mother called in hopes of getting more information as to our travel plans. To her delight she was told we had been delayed in leaving the city. They said she could probably still reach Rev. Weston at the garage where our car was being repaired.

That is where she caught us, and we made a hurried trip to the hospital's intensive care unit where the little baby was gasping, struggling to stay alive. The doctor said, "There are at least fifteen pounds of excess fluid in that little body. We can tap and remove the water, but we feel the resultant shock would terminate life."

There in that room, facing what seemed like an impossible, hopeless case, God again performed the supernatural. Yes, in answer to prayer, a miracle took place: the fluid disappeared, that little bloated body became normal, eyes opened, and little arms reached for its mommy. The Great Physician had slipped into that room, listened to a combined prayer of faith and touched a little fevered brow. He made a tiny baby whole, and just as quietly slipped away, while we mortals voiced our praise for His marvelous love, grace and power.

In later years, Dad would often display a picture he carried in his Bible, of a little girl, the wind blowing her curls as she played on the lawn of her prairie home. She was the picture of health and vitality. He'd look lovingly at that happy little face and say, "Thank you, Lord, for this testimony of your never-failing love." Dad prized that picture sent by a grateful mother. And me, well, I'd remember the collision with a streetcar that made that photo possible and whisper a quiet, "Amen."

CHAPTER FIVE

Dad in Our Home

Then there was W.G., the family man. A man's ministry is proven first in his home. Let me recount in this chapter some very real and practical lessons our family learned from a man who lived out what he preached in that pulpit.

Dad loved his family and his home. We kids, Bea, Bob and I, adored him. Each of us would proudly state in the presence of one and all that our dad was the most Christ-like person we had ever known. He lived and practiced in our home what he preached in public. One of his favorite hymns was "Be like Jesus":

> This my song
> In the home and in the throng
> Be like Jesus all day long
> I would be like Jesus.

How often in conversations, as we traveled the highways of America, he'd say, "Bill, if dad has ever said or done anything that has ever in any way impaired your faith or trust in me in any measure, please forgive me." Then, this always followed. He'd slap my knee and say these thrilling words: "I surely love you, Son, and I long, in every way, to so represent my Lord and Savior so that you, my family and loved ones, will never have any cause for embarrassment."

Just reliving now such memorable occasions is such pleasure for me. I'm certain Bob and Bea would emphatically agree with me: we remember Dad as a man who lived in an unbroken fellowship with his Lord and Master. In us, his family, he inspired faith by his way of living. We believed him. His word was as good as his bond.

Let me give you an example. My younger brother, Bob, when just a little tyke, was promised a certain gift by Dad if he'd obey and be a good boy. He had told Bob that on his next trip to Pittsburgh he'd purchase a certain toy and bring it home to him. On Dad's word alone, Bob ran out of the house and told all the kids on the hill that he had it.

Well, you know youngsters; they were big-eyed and impressed. But seeing is believing, so they said, "Let's see it, Bob."

Unabashed, Bob said, "Well, I don't have it yet but my dad's promised to get it for me."

Now unimpressed, they retorted, "Well until you get it, don't tell us you have it, because until we can see it we won't believe you."

Not to be put down, Bob answered, "Aw! You kids! I do so have it. You guys just don't know my dad."

My father in relating this story of his son's faith in him would say, "You see, beloved, my promise, my word, was as real to Bob as the gift he coveted. And, you better believe this man would rather lose an arm, and I mean literally, than to ever have failed that boy of mine, or cause his faith in his Dad to be questioned."

Then he'd proceed to make this spiritual application: We, as God's children, ought to have the same implicit, simple faith in our heavenly Father's promises and His ability to meet all of our needs. That real faith in God is when His promises are as real to us as the thing we're asking for.

Yes, Dad lived what he preached in our home, before his family. But then, as the song states, he also lived it "in the throng"—in his hometown. And that's saying something, because in a small town like Elizabeth, Pennsylvania, your business is everybody's business. There, too, Dad's testimony rang true. They knew his witness for Christ was for real. I can remember one incident that really proved Dad was what he claimed to be.

It was a scalding hot day in July, the kind where folks will say you could fry eggs on the sidewalk. Everywhere you looked there were heat waves rising from the pavement. The humidity was high, too, I mean really high! Water poured out of your pores like you'd sprung a leak. Do you get the picture? It was hot!

Well, in that steam-bath atmosphere, Dad had made a trip downtown. He parked the car in front of Cochenour and Miller's Drugstore and went shopping in Marracini's Grocery Store. From there he went to Wander's Fruit Market. When he returned with his purchases and had deposited them in the back seat, he noticed the left back tire, next to the curb, was flat. (Let me clarify something here for the benefit of those who might wonder how the left side of a car could be parked next to the curb. The explanation is simple enough: it was a one-way with parking on both sides.) To add to the problem, the curb was high right there, which meant elevating the car as high as the jack would lift in order to swing that flat tire free.

Standing in the shade of an awning projecting over the sidewalk was one of our neighbors, Mr. Jorgenson, by name. He had spotted that flat tire first, recognized our car and so had waited on the scene to see how that Preacher Weston would react when he returned and found he'd have a tire to change in that torrid weather.

Dad, unaware of anyone looking on, quietly took off his tie, rolled up his sleeves, opened the trunk and removed the jack. Dropping on his knees he shoved the jack back under the axle and began turning the inserted handle to lift the car. Without thinking, he began to whistle one of the old hymns and continued to do so throughout the whole procedure. He removed the hubcap and lugs from the wheel, replacing that flat tire with the spare. Then reversing the action on the jack, he lowered the car, put things back into the trunk and closed it. And all the time he was whistling or humming his little tune. Sure he was perspiring. His shirt now was soaked, clinging to his body. His forehead beaded with perspiration, chin dripping water.

As he opened the door of the car he turned and noticed Mr. J. Dad smiled and said, "Hello, neighbor, can I give you a lift?" When the response was a rather surly, "No," he got in, started the car and drove away.

Quite sometime later, when Mr. Jorgenson had become a Christian, he reminded Dad of this incident. Then he said, "Brother Weston, it was your undisturbed attitude in that situation, on that blistering, hot, humid July day that got to me. Had the situation been reversed, you would have found me cussin' a blue streak instead of whistling as you did. That made me realize your Christianity was for real. It was genuine, had to be, under those circumstances. And that started me thinking and really got me on the road to also becoming a Christian."

And what a dear friend Jorgenson became to the Weston household! I might inject here that mom too had a part in reaching Mr. J. for the Lord Jesus. He dearly loved homemade bread and my mom made the best homemade bread you ever slapped a tongue around. (Did you ever fuss or hassle over who would get the heel off a freshly baked loaf of bread? We did.) Anyhow, Mother would see that one loaf out of every baking would find its way up our street four doors to the Jorgensons'. What wonderful neighbors they were—dear, precious friends.

Dad, in reminiscing about this incident, would often chuckle as he'd say, "It surely had to be the Lord's doings, Son, that had me whistling that day for Jorg's benefit, because hot as it was, I sure don't think I'd have thought of it by myself."

Have you ever heard it said, "It's nobody's business how I live as a Christian"? Well, just you write this down in your memory and pull it down occasionally to look at, because if you have made a profession of faith in the Lord Jesus Christ, then it's everybody's business as to how you live and represent Him. You see, how you live speaks so loud folks can't hear what you say. And believe it, folks are watching you.

Neither my brother, Bob, nor any of our family will ever forget an experience shared with Dad at a football game. My kid brother was playing his last game as a senior for Elizabeth High School. The opposition was Clairton High, an across-the-river team, meaning the Monongahela River. It was a rivalry so intense that to clobber them in any sport was the ultimate. It would insure a successful season even if we lost all the other games on our schedule.

That Friday evening at the supper table Bob said, "Dad, it's my last game and I sure wish you and Mom could come. You haven't been able to attend any of my games this year and I know you used to attend when Bill was playing."

Dad replied, "You're right, Son. I'm sorry we missed them, but Mom and I will be there today. Mother dear, let's drop any other plans we have because tonight we should go to watch our boy play."

I was tickled to hear Dad say that, because, you betcha, I was going to be there. I've always been so proud of my brother Bob and his accomplishments. He was a crackerjack football player and he knew he could count on my support at every game I could attend.

Now to set the stage for what happened that evening, I need to give you some background. In his "Victory Hour" message on the fruit of the Spirit (Galatians 5), Dad would often say, "You can't put any fruit on the tree, but what's on the tree when you shake it will come off. And so it is in our lives, spiritually. When folks shake our tree, what's inside will come out. For example, when things go wrong, like hitting your finger with a hammer, that won't put any fruit on the tree, but it will without a doubt release what's there." Now with that setting, let's continue with our football scenario.

We're in the waning moments of the fourth quarter. Our team is getting smeared, clobbered. We'd had nothing to cheer about. Bad breaks, mistakes, fumbles, missed tackles had allowed that big Clairton football juggernaut to roll up an insurmountable score. To add insult to injury, they'd recovered another fumble well within our territory and their third-string quarterback was scrambling, looking for another receiver to launch yet another touchdown pass. He spotted his man, threw the ball, but out of nowhere came my kid brother. He leaped high in the air, caught that ball, scurried out of that end zone and ran the length of the field for a touchdown.

It was the first time all evening anything exciting had happened for our home team and the people in the stands on our side of the field erupted. Our Elizabeth High Rooters cheered themselves hoarse. Now we kids of the Weston household will all concur in this: Our Dad had a BIG voice, but that evening it became obvious to all and sundry, as suddenly our Pop boomed out over all that hubbub with a bombastic "Hal-le-lu-jah!"

Really, it was not what one expected to emanate from a rooting corps in any ballpark. Even our dear Mom, a rather meek little soul not accustomed to the goings-on in stadiums, felt that explosion was inappropriate since we weren't in church. And she immediately proceeded to nudge Dad quite vigorously. She wanted to remind him that such terminology wasn't suitable at that moment.

Dear Dad, bless his heart, simply shrugged and said to a smiling crowd that had turned to look at him after the outburst, "Well, folks, you'll have to excuse me. I just didn't know what else to shout."

Did that make an impression? You bet it did. Several people who'd been rather demonstrative, kinda simmered down with the bad language, and even a few openly apologized to the Reverend for some utterances made. Yes, it's true! What's inside will come out.

Wotta Dad! Laughing about it many times in later years, he'd say, "Well, Son, you know those folks really didn't need to apologize to me. It was the Lord they'd affronted." And I'd quietly nod my head in agreement, but thinking all the time, *That's true, Dad, but they were made God-conscious because I had a Pop whose life was a witness for his Master—even at a football game.*

For the last story in this chapter, allow me to relate my most memorable experience—one so unforgettable, so vivid and real that I can relive it at any time. As I tell this story you'll understand even better than ever why I entitled this book, "What a Dad I Had."

It was my senior year in high school when it happened. As I recall, it was following a football game and yours truly had received some undeserved accolades. Why the fellow who scores the touchdowns receives the headline billing is still a mystery to me. It's a team effort. If it weren't for those pulling guards leading interference and big guys up in that line opening up holes in the opposition's defenses big enough sometimes to drive a Mack truck through, no running back would go anywhere, period.

Anyhow, my name appeared on the sports page of our daily newspaper along with the words "Star of the Game" in big bold letters. Wow! What that can do to a fellow's ego! Inflation of another sort sets in. No hat is large enough to fit you. Then, following the head swelling, this particular malady progresses into a severe case of ingrown admiration and in its final stages, you find yourself in that delirious state of becoming so very proud of your parents for having such a wonderful son.

Well, in that cocky, self-impressed period I did a very wrong thing. No, you do not need to know what it was, and if you think you do know what it was, it was something else. Suffice it to say I was ashamed, and so delayed going home for quite a spell. I was sure my dad would hear about it and, well, I just didn't fancy facing him with egg all over my face. I never could lie to my dad. He could read me like a book.

The hour grew late and eventually there was nothing else to do but go home. When I came through the back door, into the kitchen stepped my dad. He had been waiting. I knew at a glance that he knew. There was no smile, no "congratulations, Son! Great game you played." He just quietly asked, "Is it true what I heard, Son?"

I couldn't fib. I said, "Yes, sir."

For a moment there was a hurt look and then he said, "I'm sorry, truly sorry to hear that, Bill." There was another moment of silence, then he said, "Well, c'mon, let's get on with it." With that, he turned, opened the cellar door and proceeded down the steps.

I froze. It hit me like a ton of bricks. He had a paddle down there, and oh, good grief, that's what he was going to do. Sure as thunder, he was going to spank me like some little old kid—me, a grown man. He, my dad, was going to paddle me? No way! He couldn't humiliate me like that. Everything inside me began to roil. I was suddenly so angry. Sure, I was wrong, but lick me like some little brat? Never!

Following him down those steps—I knew better than not to do so—I was clinching and unclinching my fists, doing my best to build up my courage to defend myself, to give Dad the tussle of his life. Of course, he couldn't see the reaction he'd caused because he was in front of me. But sure enough, he crossed that basement floor, turned and facing me, he picked up that paddle. Yes, sir, it was true. I just couldn't believe it. This couldn't be happening to me, his grownup son.

Suddenly, he stopped. He noticed my belligerent attitude, my gnarled fists, my white knuckles. (It's funny now how well I remember those white knuckles.) I was clinching them so tightly the blood couldn't get through.

Then these unforgettable words came from my father: "Hmmm! Look at what we have here. Gonna give Dad a hard time? Well, Son, with your size and strength I reckon you'll get in a few licks, but hear me, lad, and hear me good. You'll never see the day when you can clean Dad's plow. I'll come out on top, every time."

And you know, I knew it was so. You see, those of you who knew my Dad will remember him as Daddy Weston, the evangelist, but I remember him before he had so mellowed—a rugged lumberjack and all man! His muscles had muscles back then. He was strong!

Then it happened. The most shocking experience, the totally unexpected. As he stepped toward me and I fearfully prepared to try and defend myself, he extended that paddle toward me and said, "Take it, Son."

I didn't know what else to do, so I took it.

Unbuttoning his shirt, he slipped out of it, and turning, he bent over Mom's washtub and said, "Okay, Bill, lay it on."

Aghast at what was happening, I said, "You mean, me whip you?"

He looked up, and the hurt look in his eyes said volumes. "Bill, did you do what they say you did?"

"Yes, sir."

"Well, then, someone has to take your whipping. You misunderstood Dad's intentions. You thought I was going to paddle you again, didn't you?"

Before I could answer he continued, "No, I didn't have that in mind at all. You're a grown man, and I figure you'd like to be treated like one. Then, Son, act like a man. You did wrong. Yes, you deserve to be punished, but hear this:"—and how well I remember this part of that basement session—"I love you, Bill," he said, and then his voice broke, "I guess more than life. I reckon I'd even die for you, Son. Now, I'm gonna take your licking because One on a cross took a terrible whipping one time for me."

And so saying, he again bent that back and said, "All right, Son, lay it on!"

Dear God! I couldn't hit him.

He turned his head and so sternly said, "Bill, hit me!"

I hit him just once, not as hard as I could have, because I just couldn't; he was my dad. I saw the white welt where I'd stung those shoulders. I couldn't stand it. I threw that paddle across that cellar, heard it ricochet off the wall and then begged, pleaded, "Please, Dad, please don't do this to me. Whip me. I can't whip you. Please, Dad!"

In a moment he had me engulfed in those big arms. He hugged me so close and then began to sob. Oh, dear Lord, it just killed me! I'd never heard my dad cry like that. Finally, when he could control his voice, he held me off at arm's length, grasping me by the shoulders so tightly he almost lifted me off the floor. Then searching my eyes with his, he said, "Bill, son, don't ever hurt Dad like this again, will you? Promise me, boy."

You know my answer to that request. Never would I fail him like that again. Wotta dad I had! Even willing to take my whipping. Oh yes, in later years, I failed him and my Lord many times after that, but never in the same area that prompted that cellar session.

He used to say, "Bill, never do anything you'd be ashamed to tell Dad or Mom." Oh how I've wished, so very many times, that I'd always heeded that sage advice. I could have saved myself so many heartaches and tears of repentance as I've traveled this highway of life.

Dad's Bible

His Bible is my most prized possession. When Dad passed away there wasn't any question as to who would be given his Bible. That was a fore-gone conclusion. It was mine. We'd traveled to-gether, shared so many experiences and it was the only thing I asked for—in fact, coveted. So Mom, Bea and Bob concurred that Dad's Bible would be given to me.

Perusing its pages I find red-inked dates, little an-ecdotes, personal thoughts, messages penned in and so much more. There are expressions of praise and thanksgiving to his Lord next to some under-lined passages of Scripture. Words like, "That's for me, Lord," "Thank you, Father dear" or "Me, too, Lord." Also, next to a promise evidently made pre-cious and real at that time of reading, "Amen."

Just recently, while reading First Thessalonians 5, how very vividly I recalled his "Victory Hour" message entitled "Rules of Conduct" and this most graphic illustration. It happened in Miami, Florida, in the old Gospel Tabernacle at 33rd & 5th Ave-nue, where God had so marvelously delivered Dad. A hopeless, dying businessman, God healed him and then thrust him out into the ministry of evan-gelism. Kneeling at an altar of prayer at the conclu-

107

sion of a morning service was an elderly lady. It was obvious at first glance that her long years of suffering with asthma had thoroughly pickled her disposition. She looked like she'd been baptized in unripened persimmon juice, thus possessing the personality of an untipped waiter. When Dad approached her, noting her unpraiseworthy demeanor, he asked, "Sister, are you praising the Lord?"

With a puckered facial expression, she responded, "Young man, I'll praise the Lord when I get rid of this asthma."

Dad said, "Dear one, that's not the solution. You see, He's worthy of your praise whether you're ever delivered of your asthma or not. Praise brings the answers to our requests in prayer."

She quickly retorted, "I've been fooled too often. I've been prayed for by every preacher that has come to town to this church. Others get healed, but I guess God just doesn't want to do anything for me."

Dad quickly said, "Dear friend, bless your heart, with this type of attitude it will do us no good to pray for you."

Before he could add another word, she butted in with, "Well, all right, young man!" And so saying, she arose from the altar and made a hurried exit from the building.

I may add here that Dad was not a young man when this story happened, but I reckon this lady of seventy-some years felt she could so address him. Anyway, Dad, in watching her depart, had pangs of conscience. He felt heavyhearted and quietly asked his heavenly Father, "Dear Lord, was I too abrupt, too severe in dealing with that dear old soul? I didn't mean to offend her. Oh, please, Lord, bring her back to the meetings."

And God did just that! She returned the following morning for the "Victory Hour" service. She was kneeling again, at almost the same place as the day before. But what a change in her attitude. This time, as Dad approached, there was a quick smile and apologies for her curt answers. Then she said, "Young man, I'm so ashamed of my words and actions here yesterday. The Lord really dealt with me in my apartment last night."

Dad broke in with, "Well, I didn't sleep too well either. I really didn't mean to hurt or offend you yesterday and if I did so, please forgive me."

She smiled and quickly answered, "Thank you, young man, but you weren't at fault. It was me, my attitude. It's been all wrong. For years I've been coming for prayer and when God didn't immediately touch me, well, I got soured up in my spirit, got bitter and just plain sulked. Well, last night your words as to how He is worthy of our praise whether we're delivered or not came back to me. God began dealing with my soured-up old spirit, revealing how He'd saved me from a life of sin and was so good to me in oh, so many ways. He had spared my life many times and was even preparing a mansion for me. He showed me what an old fool I've been."

Dad, in telling this story, used to insert here: "I silently said, 'Thank you, Lord, for showing her that, because I surely couldn't have told her that.' "

Tears welled now, spilled over and ran down that beautiful, ol' wrinkled face, as she said, "I'm so ashamed and I'm here to openly confess to you and these other people, to ask His forgiveness and yours too, and I'm determined to praise my Lord the rest of my days even if I'm never delivered of this asthmatic condition."

Immediately, Dad said, "Beloved, you're ready to be anointed."

Prayer was made and she went out of the service.

What happened? Believe it, the devil doesn't give up without a real struggle. That night her asthma was worse than at any other time in her life. She thought she was going to die. Her neighbors thought she was going to die. The doctor, hurriedly summoned by her friends, came and he too thought she would expire.

Her testimony that next morning in the meeting was a never-to-be-forgotten experience for all who were there. As she stood in the aisle, rocking back and forth on her toes, hands extended toward heaven, her face a picture to behold, these words flowed across her lips and found lodgment in the hearts of every listener present: "Dear ones, God has healed me. Last night, I battled for my life. I thought I was a goner for sure. I've never had such an attack of asthma. As I gasped for air, I truly thought every breath would be my last. Neighbors and friends with me thought so too. I'm sure the doctor, bless his heart, thought he was losing another patient.

"Well, bless God, I was determined to go, if go I must, praising the Lord. So with every gulp of air I'd say, 'Thank you, Jesus! Praise the Lord!' and dear ones, about four o'clock this morning that old devil got so sick of me praising the Lord that he packed up his asthma and beat it."

What a blessed testimony! The reaction by that audience assembled was immediate and spontaneous. Shouts of "Hallelujah! Praise the Lord!" Tears of joy, laughter, even applause broke out as people celebrated the goodness, the mercy, the grace, the wonderful love of our wonderful, glorious Christ and Lord.

On the flyleaves of his Bible Dad penned in names of so many dear ones that evidently he had promised to remember in prayer, or to refresh his memory of illustrations used in his ministry. Thus, from these records I now can reach back in my mind to reproduce the following two stories, lifting them out of the past and reliving them.

One time while in meetings in Minnesota my father was being entertained in a boardinghouse. Daily he would gather with the other guests for the evening meal. Perhaps the word had gotten around that a clergyman was the newest arrival because his attempts to get acquainted with the other lodgers was totally unsuccessful. They studiously ignored him. That is, all but one—a young nurse in a hospital located a short distance away. I mention her here because she was to play an active role in this true story of God's amazing grace.

Since the hostess didn't ask him to say grace, Dad would bow his head and silently thank the Lord each evening for the food provided. He felt even his witness in this respect was unproductive since the others, ignoring him, would be chaffing, laughing, clattering dishes, filling their plates, seemingly totally unaware of his presence at the table.

Then one evening he noted that as he bowed his head this young nurse seated next to him also bowed and quietly waited for him to finish his prayer before she would help herself to the food being served. Thereafter, he had several opportunities to converse with her, to share his testimony and tell her of his ministry there in that city.

One night, late, he heard a telephone ring. Thinking the manager or one of the other guests would surely answer, he lay in his bed waiting for the ringing to cease. But no, it continued to ring on and on. Finally Dad arose, put on his bathrobe and house slippers, and went to answer it. He headed towards the stairs, the direction from which the phone kept ringing. In relating this experience Dad would often say, "I too learned a spiritual lesson from that ringing bell. When calling upon the Lord, not to give up until I got an answer because, if that telephone had quit ringing I never would've found it, since, as in this occasion, they so often tuck the phones away in some niche where it's almost impossible to find them."

As a stranger in that boarding house he didn't know where the light switches were so it meant stumbling through the dark most of the way until he finally located the phone. Upon lifting the receiver and saying "Hello," the first words that fell upon his ear were these: "Is this the house where the man of God lives who believes God answers prayer?"

Dad answered, "I don't know to whom you wish to speak, but I'm Rev. Weston and I surely know God answers prayer."

"Oh, thank God! You're the one, you're the man I want to talk to, Rev. Weston. The nurse here at the hospital told me that there was a man who lived

where she did who believed God could help us in
our trouble. My 17-year-old daughter, Nora, is dying, sir. They say there's no hope. They operated,
but her appendix had burst and peritonitis had already set in. She's in a coma and they don't think
she'll last through the night. Rev. Weston, are you
there?"

"Yes."

"Well, sir, would you please pray for my darling
girl. She's dying and we don't know God. We used
to go to church, but then we quit attending and we
never let my little girl go, not even to Sunday
school. We didn't want her to get emotionally involved with religion. We wanted her to enter the
entertainment world and be a dancer, and from our
little experience in religion we felt the church or
pastor would influence her against such wishes. But
dear God, sir, she's dying and I see things so differently now. Oh, please, Rev. Weston, pray for my
Nora."

Dad broke in on her almost hysterical monologue
assuring her he would be praying. He told her that
if Nora regained consciousness to call him and he
would immediately come to the hospital. Then he
said, "Mother, what are you going to do about your
own spiritual condition? You need to meet God too
in order to be able to join me in praying for your
daughter."

"Rev. Weston, I'll do anything you say," she said.
"Tell me how to get right with God. I do want to be
forgiven."

Over the phone Dad explained quickly the plan
of salvation. Then he told her to go back to the bedroom and commit her life to the Lord Jesus Christ

and to receive Him into her heart. She promised she would, and with tears and gratitude she said, "God bless you, Rev. Weston. I'll do as you say and you keep praying for Nora, and if she awakens I'll call you right away."

Dad returned to his room and was still on his knees in prayer when about an hour later the phone rang again. This time he was there in a minute. As he answered there was such hope in a voice that before had been so distressed. "Rev. Weston, Nora's regained consciousness and she wants you to come right away. Oh, please do come immediately and, Rev. Weston, I received Jesus into my heart, but I don't rightly know how to explain it to Nora like you did, so please hurry, sir." She then gave the number of the hospital room.

Dad dressed, summoned a cab and was taken quickly to that Catholic hospital. One of the sisters met him as he came out of the elevator. While escorting him to the room she said, "Reverend, please be very kind and gentle with Nora. She's not expected to live. There were complications, you see, after unsuccessful surgery."

Dad assured her as a servant of the Lord he couldn't be otherwise than considerate. As he entered the room, two nurses, one on either side of the bed were standing by. One was checking blood pressure. The mother, who'd been kneeling by the bed arose and was at his side instantly. "Thank you, oh, thank you, Rev. Weston, for coming. Nora, this is the minister I've been telling you about. Please listen now to what he says to you, honey."

Dad looked down into a pair of big brown eyes. Pain and fear were both registered there. He quietly told her of a Savior who loved her and would not only give her peace of heart, but also heal her sick body. She listened intently, never taking her eyes off of him and when he asked her finally if she understood and if she would like to invite the Lord Jesus to come into her heart, her response was instant. "Oh, yes, please pray for me. And show me, teach me how to pray, Rev. Weston."

Kneeling down, Dad took Nora's hand in his, prayed and then led Nora in her prayers of repentance, asking for forgiveness and inviting Jesus to come into her heart.

As they finished praying he noted both nurses had been kneeling and praying also. What happened? The Lord Jesus became Nora's Savior and Great Physician, too. Her face was a picture to behold. The death pallor was gone, that face that seemed drained of color was now flushed and a divine life was being transfused through her body. She took on new strength and asked the nurses to prop her up in bed. They immediately did so. She said, "Mother, I'm hungry, and you know what I want? A tomato sandwich."

The one nurse hurriedly left the room. She explained later she'd gone to her nurses' station to call the resident doctor about Nora's request. He sleepily replied, "Oh, sure, give her anything she wants. This is a little emotional upsurge, and she's dying, so grant her request, but of course."

Well, to their surprise she ate her sandwich and instead of dying, proceeded to get better and within a week was released from the hospital. As a result of Nora's miraculous deliverance, her entire family embraced true Christianity and her pastor told my father at a later council gathering, he wished he could have a dozen families like Nora's. They were tremendous soul-winners and workers for our Lord.

From John 14, I remember one of the sweetest illustrations of how God provides for His children. It was one I never tired of hearing my Father use during "Victory Hour" sessions. This true story happened in a little bungalow on the outskirts of Winnipeg, Canada. As I recall, Rev. George Blackett was the pastor whose faith was truly enlarged by this experience.

My father and I had stayed with Brother Blackett and his wife in their home in Toronto when he was serving as the pastor there at the Old Christy Street Tabernacle of The Christian and Missionary Alliance. He was truly a man of God and so vitally involved in the affairs of his congregation. No matter when the call came this faithful shepherd of the flock was always available to minister to the sheep of his pasture.

One evening he had returned to the parsonage, bone weary from a long day of counseling, visiting at the hospitals and calling on others in their homes. He ate his supper and decided to retire early. While listening in his bedroom to radio weather reports he learned of a new winter blizzard moving in on that prairie city. His thoughts were suddenly centered on a dear elderly couple living in a little cottage way out in the suburbs. He hadn't seen them for quite awhile. They were unable to come to the services anymore, as the husband was semi-invalid, bedfast most of the time. His dear old wife was faithfully caring for their needs.

Finally, with his feelings for their safety continuing to plague his thoughts, he got out of bed.

Getting dressed and donning his big mackinaw coat, he prepared to battle his way through the swirling, drifting snowstorm to that little hovel just beyond the city limits. Several times he was tempted to discontinue this errand of mercy as that winter blizzard increased in its intensity. Heavy wind squalls soon made the roads in many places impassable with huge drifts. And so he had to make several detours in order to find a street where he could get through. A few hundred feet from their home he had to leave his car and proceed on foot.

Covering his face with his scarf, he plodded those last yards to the gate, up a short walk, toward a cheery little light beaming out of the window next to the front door. Peering through that partially frosted window he could faintly see that cozy little room that served as living, dining and bedroom. The old gentleman was propped up in bed, clasping the hand of his sweetheart, as she, sitting in the rocking chair beside that bed was singing,

> Be not dismayed whate'er betide,
> > God will take care of you
> Beneath His wings of love abide,
> > God will take care of you.

He listened on as she sang the chorus,

> God will take care of you,
> > thro every day, o'er all the way
> He will take care of you,
> > God will take care of you.

As the strains of that glorious old hymn continued to fill that little room, our pastor friend, with tears now welling in his eyes, noted the little stove

117

in the center of the room and was jolted into action. Forcing himself to leave that beautiful scene, he plodded through the snow to the back of that little house. Opening the door to a sort of lean-to shed adjoining the house, that served as the coal cellar, his flashlight revealed an empty bin. A broom had been used to sweep up even the smallest crumbs of that fuel. The coal bucket he'd seen next to the stove was also empty.

A cold chill, not caused by that winter storm, swept up and down his spine. "Oh, dear Lord, it's even worse than I expected," he whispered. A sort of panic gripped him as he realized with the lateness of the hour all the coal dealers would be closed, their trucks garaged for the night.

As he turned, his coat sleeve caught the handle of a shovel leaning against the wall and sent it clattering to the floor. Knowing the noise would surely startle his aged friends, he quickly opened the backdoor and made his presence known. That little mother was on her feet immediately and with surprise registered in her voice, but a warmth in her smile, she said, "Daddy, it's the pastor. Bless your heart, dear, what in the world brings you clear out here through this horrible blizzard? Oh my! You must be about frozen. You're covered with snow. Here, let me take your coat. I'll shake it off, hang it up and get you a quick cup of hot tea." Then again, before he could answer, she said, "We're so happy to see you, but dear, dear, what in the world brought you clear out here on such a terrible, blustery, stormy night?"

Still standing, although she was insisting he be seated on a chair which she had hurriedly pulled into a position near the stove, he finally broke into the conversation. "No, dear ones, I can't be seated. It's so very late." He hurriedly described his feelings of concern for their safety which had motivated his visit. "I don't know where in the world I'll be able to get coal for you at this time of the evening. Perhaps you had better just bundle up good and return with me to the parsonage."

The dear old couple quickly declined. "Daddy couldn't possibly be moved," she said, adding cheerily, "Pastor, we've placed our order for coal with our heavenly Father and He's always on time."

Brother Blackett wanted to be so convinced, but with the bucket by the stove also empty, and all the coal dealer supply houses now closed, he tried to convince them to change their minds. But those precious old saints wouldn't be swayed. The old gentleman on the bed joined with his wife in insisting that he sit down and visit a spell. "We've ordered the coal from the Father, pastor, and like you've always told us, He never fails. Amen!"

Then he saw that dear old lady had a cup of steaming tea extended toward him. He took it while she hustled to the cupboard to fill a dish with several types of home-baked cookies. Because he didn't know what else to do, the pastor finally sat down like they had been insisting. He sat just on the edge of the chair, however, as he was trying to come up with a plan for getting them the fuel they needed to weather the storm.

Noting his continued lack of ease, the lady said, "Pastor, as we told you, Daddy and I ordered the coal during our devotions, so now don't you worry none. And besides you can see that little stove is still red hot."

He had just noted that, and also the open Bible lying on the bed, when suddenly, the conversation was interrupted by the roar of a big chugging motor. In a moment there was a heavy knock on the door which Grandma hastened to answer.

There was a big, burly character, stamping his feet, nose cherry red, blowing on his hands. The moment he spoke, all concern was immediately erased, tension was gone. "Hi, Grandma! Wow! It's cold! I planned to have this coal delivered to you earlier today, and didn't, so I couldn't put my rig away until I got out here. Been awhile since I've been here so I imagine that old coal bin of yours is mighty close to being empty. So, I'll just quick unload and get back to town because this storm is sure getting bad."

She quickly assured him he was right on time, thanked him repeatedly and closed the door. Then turning to her pastor she smiled at him, wrinkling her nose and winking as she did so. "You see?" she whispered. "I told you so."

In sharing this experience, our pastor friend said the old couple's faces were beaming with confidence in proving their heavenly Father's protective care. Suddenly, he said he felt very ashamed for the littleness of his own faith. There was only one thing left to do. Kneeling humbly beside their bed, hands clasping theirs, he quietly thanked God for His faithfulness, and asked forgiveness for his anxiety, impatience, and lack of believing faith. Then, recommitting those dear ones to the loving care of his heavenly Father, he said his goodbyes and headed back for the parsonage.

These thoughts were voiced audibly as he drove through that winter storm: "Father, never ever let me forget the lesson learned this night. Help me, like those saintly people, to so rest in your abiding love that never again will I question your ability to supply all of our needs through your riches in glory by Christ Jesus."

Our pastor friend then added, "The moral to this wonderful, true story of God's protective care is this: We're not to fuss, fret or worry about the bin nor buckets. If we'll keep our little stove (our heart) red hot, our loving heavenly Father, who is so aware of all of our needs, even before we ask or call, will surely see to the filling of the bin and the buckets from His limitless storehouse on high."

From Dad's underscoring of Luke 2:5 in his Bible, I lift this very graphic illustration from a sermon he entitled, "Bread at Midnight." We had just purchased a new Chevrolet four-door sedan. You all know how you treat a brand new car. It smells so good, you even polish the paint with your coat sleeve. That is, until after its exposure to the first rain and sloppy roads. Then, that first love wanes a spell and you aren't quite so particular about dust and dirt accumulating. Our inaugural trip in that Chevy was from Elizabeth, Pennsylvania to Atlanta, Georgia, approximately 600 miles. Believe me, that trip to that southern metropolis I'll never forget. Because the car was new, we had to drive no more than 30 miles per hour for the first 1,000 miles, and no more than 50 for the first 10,000 miles. I thought that trip would never end.

We finally arrived and a few days later we were following the flow of traffic on one of the major avenues of Atlanta, when out of a side street came an old jalopy, which ran full tilt into our spanking new automobile. It seemed the driver, a young man in his teens, had totally ignored the stop sign on that corner. However, it proved out later, he'd seen it, but the brakes in that old heap no longer responded to such pedal pressures. So, the right front end of our car became his brakes.

The impact truly rocked us but, thank the Lord, didn't knock us over. However, we occupants were suddenly and unceremoniously reintroduced to each other, as I found myself trying to occupy my father's side of the front seat.

Fortunately, neither of us suffered any serious injuries. Stoved up a mite, yes, and for the next few days, we got reacquainted with some muscles we'd been unaware of for some time. They just sort of indicated their disapproval with some rather spectacular twinges, thus letting us know they hadn't exactly appreciated such sudden log-jamming procedures. I believe my right collar bone thought for a moment about getting out of joint, but then decided to pop back into place, thus negating the usage of splint or sling.

Naturally we enquired of each other as to any injuries sustained and then, as quickly as possible, clambered out of the car to survey the damages. By now a crowd was gathering and their faces revealed what we already feared. What a mess! Without being descriptive, I'll just let your imagination conjure up the scene that was registering in the photographic department of my mind.

Then, what happened next really disjointed my nose a bit. The young fellow who had caused this catastrophe was a standing there cussing up a storm. It quickly dawned on me that the recipient of those awful words was obviously me. I was about to get in my two-cents' worth, when Dad came around the front of our car to remonstrate with him. That kid now turned that undesirable language in my father's direction. Well, now, cussing me was one thing, but coloring the atmosphere blue towards my pop caused my righteous indignation to soar. I was just plumb seeing Russian—red, to you. I felt like decking him and, oh yes, I could have. You see, during my high school years, I used to train for athletic endeavors with a black friend of mine, by the name of Tiger Joe Randall. He was a "tee-rif-fic" boxer—licked the welter-weight champion of the world in a non-title scrap in Pittsburgh. Tiger Joe taught me the manly art of self-defense, so I repeat, oh yes, I could have floored that young'un, even beaten the bejabers out of him.

Now, as I reminisce, I'm so glad I didn't follow through on that enraged impulse because wouldn't that have looked good in a newspaper column: "Evangelist Decks Kid." As it turned out, we didn't have to react at all to his blasphemous routine because one of Atlanta's finest, who'd been patrolling that particular beat, had been an observer of the whole affair. He came running up just then, and, you know, the appearance of that officer lowered that lad's hotheaded temperature to subzero.

The policeman's first words did it. "Cut the foul language, Son," he said. "I saw this whole thing. You ran that stop sign. You're fortunate to be alive.

You could've plowed into that truck loaded with steel girders instead of this car and you'd have been pulverized. Let's see your license."

Wouldn't ya know it. That lad didn't have any license. In fact, at 15 he was not even old enough to have one. And there were no license plates on that jalopy, it had no brakes, and on top of that, it was a stolen car. The officer just shook his head in disbelief. Then he escorted that youngster away.

He returned to get information from us and to notify us that we should appear at the city courthouse the morning of such-and-such a day and date. Time elapsed and on that day, early in the morning, my father aroused me from nodville and enquired if I remembered what day it was? I was unusually sharp and replied, "It's Monday."

He smiled and said, "So it is, Son, but that's not what I meant. Do you know where we're to be this morning?"

Really, I'd forgotten, but before I could answer he continued. "Bill, we're to appear in court today, and Son, Dad didn't sleep too well last night and I'd like to have you pray with me."

Right away I was anxious. "Are you sick, Dad?" I asked.

His reply reassured me. "No, Son, I'm not ill, but I've been doing a lot of thinking about that lad who hit our car. I haven't loved him very much nor have I prayed for him as I should've either. You see, Son, the reason he cursed us out was because he doesn't know our Savior and, well, we're representing our Lord, and I just wanted you to pray with me, and for me, that I might have the proper love for that boy when we appear in that courtroom today."

My first thoughts were, *Wow! How like my Dad. Always so considerate of others with their burdens and problems.* But my reply was, "Boy, Dad, if you need prayer I *really* need it, because I wanted to deck that kid for cursing like that and especially so when he turned on you."

Again, an understanding smile and then he knelt by my bed. I crawled out and, kneeling beside him, we prayed together, asking our heavenly Father to fill our hearts with His kind of love for a young man who was about to face an earthly judge and needed us as friends. I don't cry very easily. It's just not my makeup, but God allowed tears to flow during that early hour prayer time and our attitudes experienced a complete reversal.

As we entered the foyer of that courthouse in downtown Atlanta, a little woman approached us. She seemed to sense who we were and extending her hand toward my dad, she said, "Are you, by any chance, Rev. Weston?" When Dad nodded, there were immediate tears.

She implored us to be merciful. "Rev. Weston, my boy was wrong in what he done, but it's the first time he's ever been in trouble, sir, and all this week he hasn't left the house. Wouldn't go to school, he's so scared and so ashamed for what he did. He's only fifteen years old, Rev. Weston, and I'm so fearful that the judge will send him to the stockade. Oh, sir, there are such bad men in that place. I just can't bear to think of my son being exposed to prison life. We don't have any money, but Rev.

Weston, I'll try to get a job to pay you back for the damage done to your car."

I'll never forget that mother's plaintive voice and the anguish registered on her face. There were deep shadows beneath those eyes that were overflowing wells. And tired lines on her forehead betrayed a lack of sleep. She was a real mom pleading for understanding and mercy for her boy.

She told us too that her husband wouldn't come along that morning. He was too angry and had spouted off about how kids nowadays are all getting too big for their britches. Headstrong, he called it, won't listen to nobody, don't appreciate how good they've got it. Maybe some time in a stockade might just be the dosage needed to straighten the kid out.

From all this that she reported, it was obvious her husband wasn't about to show up in that courtroom. He had told her, "He's disgraced us, so now let him take his medicine."

That, of course, was the male parent speaking. Sure, he was hurt and embarrassed, but his son needed him. But at least that boy's mom was there. You see, she'd gone into the valley of the shadow of death to bring that young'un into this world and nobody could keep her away from her son's side, no matter what.

Dad reassured her of our desire to help them. He told her we wouldn't be pressing any claims and since we were the injured party in this case, we would try to persuade the judge to temper any sentence to the limit with mercy.

The case was called. We told our stories and it really didn't look good for the lad. We didn't bend the truth. Some seem to think that under some conditions it doesn't really hurt to add a little white lie if it will help the situation. But, you know, I've never ever seen a color scheme for lying. Usually when you tell one little white lie, you have to tell eleven or twelve great big black ones to back it up. And then you have to remember what you said. Telling the truth never necessitates a good rememberer because the story remains constant.

Just as the judge was about to pass sentence, my father arose from his chair and approached the bench. "Your Honor, could I have a further word before you pass sentence?"

"Surely, Reverend," the judge said. "If you have something further to say that is relevant to this case, this is the time and place for it."

My Dad thanked him and then launched this statement. "Your Honor, we are the injured party in this case but, as I've already indicated, we are not going to press charges nor try to collect any damages from this young man or his family. We understand it's the boy's first criminal offense and his mother has assured us that her son has been so very repentant, so very sorry for his actions of last week. A falling out and a misunderstanding with his father precipitated his anger, resulting in the taking of that car from a parking lot, as a means of transportation, in his plans to run away from home.

"It was wrong, sir, and this young man has admitted that, and has asked all involved, including those present in this court, to please forgive him. We have accepted his statement of sorrow for his actions and have granted our forgiveness.

"Now, Your Honor, I'm requesting that you please temper justice with a great amount of mercy. Perhaps, if I may so suggest, since I'm not competent in such court procedures, could you possibly see fit to sentence this young man and then suspend such sentence, paroling him to the care of his parents? Maybe, if need be, have him even report to you or this court, or a parole officer once a month or as often as you would deem necessary. Because of his age and the fact that this is his first offense, and his promise to his parents, to me and to this court, that he's learned his lesson well and won't repeat same, would you, Your Honor, Sir, please forfeit any sentencing requiring an incarceration period in prison?"

I wish you could have seen that old judge's face. It was a mask. No emotions were revealed, but I knew, I guess by looking at his eyes, that he was truly impressed by that Preacher Weston's plea for mercy. He leaned forward in his swivel chair. Dad was standing close to the bench and I think the judge's next action sort of caught him by surprise.

Extending his hand, with index finger pointed toward my father, that old judge began to wiggle his finger right under my Dad's sneezing machinery and then he spoke these words: "Reverend, are you a preacher of righteousness?"

Dad's reaction: "I certainly trust so, sir."

Then slowly, with every word emphasized, the judge said, "Well then, suppose you tell me and this court, why you, a minister of righteousness, are trying to interfere with justice."

Bless his old heart, he asked for it. And my daddy gave it to him. Now I've heard my old pop wax elo-

quent on many occasions, but that day in the court
room, he plumb outdid himself. God love him, he
became an orator of the William Jennings Bryan
stature. By the time he'd finished painting, so vividly in word pictures, a Cross on a lonely hillside,
you felt you had been there, reviewing that whole
Mount Calvary scene with the blood actually flowing from the lacerated back and riven side of the
Savior of mankind. His description of that crucifix-
ion scene that meant man's redemption back off
the auction block of sin, took its toll on all assembled in that courtroom.

All eyes were riveted, focused on a big six-foot
evangelist caught up in his message of a glorious,
victorious Christ. His audience seemed transfixed
as he finally concluded with these words that no
one present would forget: "Your Honor, if I had received justice I'd be in hell, a lost soul, condemned
forever. But God so loved me, sir, and loves you
too, Judge, that He gave His only Son to pay sin's
ransom price to set sinners like you and me free. I
stood before His bar of judgment, a guilty condemned man, and He tempered justice with oh, so
much mercy and because of that extended mercy
I'm eternally indebted to my heavenly Father.

"You see, Your Honor, we all need mercy. The Bible says, 'We all have sinned.' 'We all like sheep
have gone astray.' Who in this courtroom would
dare stand and say they'd never sinned, never broken God's laws, never committed acts they were
ashamed of? So, sir, I'm pleading for mercy for a
boy, only fifteen years of age, still so immature in
his knowledge and recognition of what constitutes
sin and right and wrong."

For a moment, when he'd finished speaking, that courtroom was as silent as a turkey farm the day after Thanksgiving. And that old judge, who had at first seemed so gruff, so stern, so austere, so unbending—with a mane of red hair that wouldn't lie down east, west, north or south; whose big red nose embraced some kinda large horn-rimmed glasses that he seemed to be peering over instead of through—well, first appearances are deceiving. There, sitting on the bench, was a thoroughly mellow old codger who evidently, even though it was August, had suddenly caught a summer cold. His eyes had puddled up and were leaking and he found it necessary to extract his handkerchief and blow his nose vociferously. No, he just wasn't at all the tough old nut I'd thought him to be.

As he shoved his chair back and arose, he started to speak. These are the words that started flowing across his lips: "Preacher, I never in all of my years on the bench—and they are many—have ever heard a more eloquent plea on behalf of a defendant. I'm proud to know you, sir, and will never forget your presentation. Furthermore, I'm going to grant your request. Young man, approach the bench."

That dear old judge took his turn in waxing eloquent, and that he was, for the next few moments. He told that young fellow that he'd had it in mind to deal quite harshly with him due to five counts against him. He even became a preacher, too, for a spell, as he reminded the boy that the Bible says to honor your father and mother. His closing words we'll never forget. "I'm granting Rev. Weston his request. I'm sentencing you to only one year, suspending that sentence and paroling you only to the care of your parents for that one-year period. If you have no further trouble or occasion necessitating a reappearance in this court, you'll not have to pay. Case dismissed."

With tears flowing, that young fellow thanked the judge and ran into the arms of an overjoyed mother. Then, how profuse their thanks to us. He cried all over my shoulder as I hugged him. And his dear old mom, well, I thought she would shake Dad's arm plumb out of the socket. In a little side room they listened to the plan of salvation, and were so eager to receive the Lord Jesus Christ. They knelt and invited the Savior to come in and take up residency within their hearts. And we, the Westons, father-and-son evangelistic team, had the blessed privilege of sharing the Living Bread with two dear people who just moments before were facing a midnight hour in their lives.

As we left that courthouse they were on our arms, both still weeping, still thanking us for being so kind to them. As we parted to go our separate ways, Dad and I were walking on cloud nine. How often, in later years, reliving that courtroom experience, we praised our God for melting our hearts through that early morning prayer session. He replaced what could've been the fleshly desire to go to that confrontation for our pound of flesh, with His heaven-sent desire to present understanding and love instead.

"God works in such mysterious ways His wonders to perform." The proof of that statement is borne out in the following unforgettable story, which was Dad's closing illustration in his message entitled, "Bread at Midnight." After the Scripture lesson (Luke 2:1-13) was read, there followed this six-point outline on what is not necessary in the production of a successful prayer ministry.

1. There is no age limit in becoming an intercessor in prayer.
2. There is no time limit in becoming an intercessor in prayer.
3. There is no place nor circumstance where prayer cannot be offered.
4. There are no educational requirements to successful praying.
5. There are no language barriers.
6. There is no crowd limit conditional to a successful prayer meeting.

Apt illustrations accentuated each point. Then my father would relate this very graphic story that found its setting in the closing years of his earthly ministry.

In my lumber business days there was a man who used to come by my office quite often to purchase carload after carload of heavy timber, to be used in shoring up the roof through a labyrinth of underground mining tunnels. He was the owner of a coal mine. His name was Mr. Bennett. Because of this close association through business dealings, Mr. Bennett and I became very good friends on a business level. Socially we were poles apart. Our paths went in opposite directions.

Mr. B. was a big, gruff, hard-nosed man, given over to language not usable in Sunday school or advisable at church functions. He never allowed himself, nor his family, to be exposed to anything religious or Bible-oriented. Our friendship, business-wise, continued through the years until after my marvelous healing experience and restoration back to life. I believe he was glad God healed me, but when I later dedicated my life to the ministry of evangelism and began to preach, our longtime friendly relationship dissolved.

For some unknown reason Mr. Bennett had an aversion to preachers. He would have absolutely nothing to do with any men of the cloth. Somewhere, somehow, some clergyman must have riled this man because his bitterness and hatred toward ministers was very obvious. Thus, when I too embraced a similar calling, he put me automatically in the same category with all the rest of those despised parsons. His attitude toward me and my family changed drastically. His language became abusive and he totally disassociated himself from any further contacts with the Weston household.

Our homes were in the same neighborhood. In a small town it's pretty difficult to avoid chance meetings, but he'd evade even the pleasantries of conventional greetings by crossing to the other side of the street to save speaking to me or mine. He said some pretty unkind things that hurt, of course, but the Lord gave me the needed grace and wisdom not to retaliate.

Then his daughter became very ill. Within just a short time doctors despaired of her chances for recovery. My daughter, Beatrice, had gone to school with Sara. Bea, precious Christian girl that she is, concerned over her former school chum's lack of any knowledge of the Lord Jesus Christ and His glorious plan of salvation, went to visit Sara in the hospital. Though near death she rebuffed my daughter's attempts to tell her the simple old gospel story, reminding her that her dad didn't believe in that religious stuff and she was too sick to listen.

She wanted Bea to leave. My, the influence of an ungodly father! Imagine, in a dying condition and frightened as she was of death and yet, adamant in her refusal to hear words that could mean life.

Later, at family altar, we prayed that God might intervene and change her attitude so she would permit an audience with someone who could lead her to the Savior. God answered that request. With His leading we returned with our daughter to that hospital. When we got to Sara's room, she received us graciously. After speaking with her, that precious girl, who didn't know how to pray, followed us word for word in a penitent's prayer, asking forgiveness and inviting the Lord Jesus to please come into her heart. The transformation was miraculous. Her assurance of salvation was immediate. Shortly afterwards a redeemed soul left that emaciated body for a permanent residency in heaven. What a glorious result!

A few weeks later my son, Bill, and I were conducting a revival meeting at the Alliance church in McKeesport, Pennsylvania. Sunday evening, Mr. B., dressed in his Sunday best, came into his living room where his wife was seated reading the newspaper. Surprised to see him dressed up, she asked the obvious question: "Where are you going?"

His reply thoroughly shocked her as you can well imagine. "I'm going down to McKeesport to hear Weston preach."

"*What?*" she exclaimed. "*You* going to *church?*"

"All right! All right!" he said. "I guess I deserve that, but you were there when our Sara died. You know as well as I do she was different, wasn't afraid to die, and it was all because of that visit by Weston and his daughter, Bea. So, well, I feel I owe it to him, because of Sara, to go and hear him preach and to tell him how much I appreciated what he did for our girl."

Mrs. Bennett, at his suggestion, hurriedly got ready and the two of them drove the eleven miles, or better, to our Alliance church located at 5th and Market Streets in McKeesport, Pennsylvania.

I will never forget that Sunday evening service. As I entered the lobby and looked through the doorway into the main auditorium, there, seated next to the aisle on the right hand side of the church, on the back pew, was Mr. Bennett. I could hardly believe my eyes, but yes, it was my former big coal miner friend. No question or doubt about that.

Well, as I stood there for the moment pleasantly shocked, my heavenly Father quietly spoke to me. He suggested that as I entered the sanctuary I was to put my arm around Mr. Bennett's shoulders and let him know how very pleased I was to see him in the house of the Lord. My reaction was immediate. This was such an unreasonable suggestion, no matter what or who had generated it. "Wait a minute, Father," I said. "That's Mr. B., and I know his violent temper, his uncontrollable flare-ups. He hates preachers, church, and now, even me because I'm in the ministry."

To do such a foolish, awkward thing as to put my arm across his shoulder and then utter such words would most certainly be inappropriate—ridiculous even—and entirely out of order. He would surely be embarrassed. It was hard to tell just what he'd do, but he would probably storm out of the place. You see, I had to tell the Lord these things because He didn't know them.

Several other thoughts and statements were also registered in that brief moment of panicked prayer.

But, you know, my heavenly Father refused to listen to my suggestions. He just quietly reiterated that I follow through on His first request. In fact, He was impressively insistent that I be obedient.

I prayed again, saying, "Well, Lord, if you haven't changed your mind"—and He hadn't—"well then, all right. If you want me to make a fool of myself and maybe cause a real disturbance, I'll do as you say, only you've got to help me." He quietly assured me that He would. All of this controversy transpired in the few seconds I stood there looking unbelievingly at a massive pair of shoulders on the man who had turned from friend to enemy.

As I approached his seat, God overwhelmed my heart with His love for that big fellow. I did as He had bid me do. I slipped my arm around those shoulders, gave a hug, and my voice broke with emotion as I said, "God bless you, Mr. Bennett. I'm so glad to see you in the house of the Lord." I lifted my arm, but not before I felt that big body tremble. Then, light and happy of heart, I proceeded to the pulpit area.

At the conclusion of my message I called for my son, Bill, to lead in the song of invitation, "Just As I Am." But before we could sing, Mr. Bennett arose and stepped into the aisle. I thought perhaps he was going to leave the church, but instead, he turned and came weeping to an altar of prayer. What a tremendous conversion experience! What a complete reversal in a personality, as God, through His tenderness and love, completely transformed that coal miner's life.

Not long afterward, Mother and I were celebrating our golden wedding anniversary. For fifty years that precious little woman had shared by my side and how dearly I loved her. It was quite an affair our children planned. Our little home on Center Avenue in Elizabeth, Pennsylvania was crowded with neighbors and friends helping us celebrate this very festive and momentous occasion.

Mr. B. was there too and he requested that sometime during the course of the evening's activities, he might have the privilege of sharing his testimony. As I recall, he said, "Will, I've told these folks in this town for years that there wasn't any God and they all know what a rough, ungodly person I've been. It would take me forever to go to them all personally to apologize and, well, I'd surely appreciate the opportunity to tell all of these people about the change in my whole outlook on life. So, if you think it would be appropriate and you can find the time to fit me into the program, I'd surely be much obliged, Will."

You can believe we found the right time; it was right then. Calling to the many neighbors gathered in our back yard and getting the attention of those in our home, I asked them all to please be quiet for a moment. I told them, "Neighbor Bennett wants to share something with us all."

He stood then in the back doorway, and speaking loudly enough for all to hear, he related his story of how God had so wonderfully changed his life. First, he apologized for the years he'd lived such a wanton life of sin, lying to them, telling all and sundry that there wasn't any God or anything to this religious business. It was an amazed audience, to be sure, who listened as he shared his new-found faith in the Lord Jesus Christ.

Then finally, he spoke these words that were so unforgettable for me and mine. "And neighbors, the reason I'm a Christian is because this man here, Will Weston, loved me."

Surprised, I hastened to break in. "Oh, wait a minute, Brother Bennett. It wasn't me," I said, "it was God that loves you."

He responded with a broad smile. "Oh yes, Brother Weston, neighbors," he said, "I know God loved and loves me, but He had to have an arm I could feel. That happened when you came into the church that evening, Will, and put your arm around me and hugged me. When you said, "God bless you, Mr. Bennett. I'm so glad to see you in the house of the Lord," your voice broke and at the same time everything inside of me let go. Inwardly I cried out, "Oh, God, after the vile and foul way I've treated this man, to now have him act that way toward me, there has to be something to this religious bit. Please God, whatever Will has, I want too." And Brother Weston, neighbors, something suddenly overwhelmed me. I'm sure I got saved right then and there in that back seat. I never did hear a word you preached that night, but when you had the folks stand to sing I just felt impelled to respond and so I came to the front of that church and to that altar."

What an impact was made on visiting friends and guests that evening!

After citing this true story of God's abundant grace and wonderful redeeming love, Dad would close the service by saying,

Dear ones, we're living in a midnight hour. Millions are wandering in the wilderness of sin, hungering and thirsting for they know not what.

Discouraged, distressed, heartbroken people long-
ing for someone to love, to care for their souls.

Would you be willing, Christian friend, to loan
God an arm? To reach those He longs to win
through a similar display of His love through you?
He has no other hands but ours to lovingly do His
bidding. No other feet but yours and mine to give
him transportation to that neighbor down the
street, to that sick one in the hospital. No one else
to carry Him and His message to those who need
to feed on the Living Bread. No other lips but ours
through which to share the good news of His love,
mercy and forgiveness. Beloved, let's be involved
in getting "Bread" at this midnight hour in our
world's history.

After reading this story I believe you'll agree that
we Weston kids had quite a Dad.

CHAPTER SEVEN

Dad's Homegoing

My dad is in heaven. I couldn't be more certain of anything than this. And I am sure it was an abundant entrance into the Celestial City for my father, W.G. Weston.

He'd been in a little town near Erie, Pennsylvania for meetings. I believe it was Union City. As I recall, he was being entertained in the home of the pastor. The first evening there he suffered a very severe and painful injury to his right hand. A chair on which he was seated overturned and in trying to break his fall, his hand hit something sharp resulting in an ugly, jagged cut, requiring fifteen to seventeen stitches. That dear pastor friend quickly tried to administer first aid to staunch the flow of blood and then rushed my father to the nearest emergency center for help. As I recall, they found no one there capable of handling his case so they hurriedly traveled on to a hospital some several miles away where they finally attended to his wound.

Later that evening he called home. Not wanting to alarm Mother or Bea he didn't mention the accident. His conversation: "Dear ones, since I'm so close to home, rather than write this week I'll just call you each evening." That was my dad. He knew he'd be unable to write with his hand so badly injured, but he also knew Mom looked forward to his daily letters. So, long distance calls were his way of saving his loved ones undue concern over his injury problem.

You see, when he was away in meetings, Dad was very faithful in his correspondence. You should have seen a sample of his handwriting. His penmanship, the old-fashioned Palmer Method, was beautiful. He taught that style of writing in earlier years as a schoolmaster, just out of college. He and Mother were lovers all their lives, and always at the bottom of those newsy letters about people, the meetings and other events, he would add Xs and Os, which anyone back then would have known meant "hugs 'n' kisses." With today's pattern of living, a letter with X's at the bottom could well mean you've been double-crossed.

Following that week of meetings, my sister, Bea, traveled to the Pittsburgh airport to meet Dad. She told me later, "Bill, I was heartsick when I saw him. He was actually ashen gray in color and was walking so slowly, lugging that big suitcase of his. I ran toward him. 'Dad, what in the world's happened to you?' I asked."

Trying to play down his physical condition he replied, "Bea, dear, I suffered a little accident to my hand last week. Lost quite a bit of blood and just haven't quite recouped as yet." During the ride home he admitted the injury and soreness had made the previous week a very difficult one, a real trial of faith.

Usually, a week of rest at home revitalized Dad and, like Paul the Apostle, he would be raring to go on his next preaching mission. However, that week, instead of regaining strength, he seemed to grow more weary. Bea, noting his condition, suggested she call the pastor where he was to hold his next series of meetings and explain that Dad would be unable to come.

His reaction to the suggestion was kind but firm. "Oh no, dear, don't do that," he said. "I've never canceled a meeting in my entire ministry and I'm sure I'll be able to keep this assignment."

But, at the end of that week, his strength had further waned and finally, reluctantly—very reluctantly, I should add—he permitted my sister, Bea, to call and cancel those services. Those meetings were scheduled for the last week in April 1964.

When my dear old dad had to cancel his first meeting in thirty-eight years of ministry, and thus also had to cancel his speaking engagement for the divine healing service at the annual council of The Christian and Missionary Alliance, something let go inside him. He tucked his feet into bed and like the patriarchs of old, gave up the ghost and decided to go home.

The next three months, we, his family, will never forget. From the time God had raised him up from a deathbed at age forty-four Dad had lived on divine life. Not even an aspirin crossed his lips. The Lord God was his Healer and Life Giver. He possessed such a simple, childlike faith. Sure, he'd had many physical testings and trials, but always his God was there to heal and deliver him.

No one, but no one, possesses the vocabulary large enough to possibly describe the hatred I have for the devil because of the severe, unrelenting, testing time to which he subjected my precious old dad during those next two months. He was so weary of mind and body, and the enemy attacked viciously, walking all over him with hobnailed boots, assailing him like he did Job. Satan did his best to convince Dad God had forsaken him, that all was lost—he was lost, his children were lost.

The darkness of the pit invaded our home. What mental anguish and torment was then visited upon a tired, worn and now fragile old warrior of the faith. While Dad was so weakened physically, Satan besieged him with taunting lies, constantly assailing his thinking processes.

Those who knew my father and his ministry, his rugged character and his deep unwavering faith in God will hardly believe this, but it happened. He drew the curtains, darkening his room, crawled into bed and shut himself off from his loved ones.

I'll never, ever forget the day I arrived home and entered that room. Instead of seeing the usual welcoming smile and hearing familiar words I always expected—"Hi, ol' pal"—there was my dad, bereft of joy, lying in darkness, despair written in every line of his tired old face. I immediately raised the blinds and pushed the curtains aside to let the sunshine in. Then taking him in my arms, I cried, "Dad, what in the world's going on here?" And before I could say more, he was weeping, cradled in my arms.

It was a rough week, and then one evening—PRAISE GOD FOR EVERMORE—the darkness was finally dispelled and God's glorious sunlight filled every nook and cranny of that old homestead at 239 Center Avenue, Elizabeth, Pennsylvania.

We had brought Dad downstairs. Bea and I were sitting with him in that little sun parlor bedroom, while Mother was busying herself in the kitchen trying to concoct something that would perk up Dad's appetite and tempt him to eat and thus gain strength.

On this trip home, I'd flown in from the West Coast. While there, I had attended one of Phil Kerr's Big Monday Night musicals in the Pasadena Civic Auditorium. Audrey Meier had just written her new chorus entitled, "His Name Is Wonderful." Her choral group presented it that evening.

As I listened, my heart was thrilled and blessed and I thought, "This has to be one of the greatest, finest, most God-inspired pieces of music ever composed." Along with that great crowd assembled I too learned that lovely song, tucked it away in my blessing cabinet, already planning to teach it to others wherever I'd have meetings.

It became my favorite of all gospel choruses and here's the reason why. I asked Dad if he'd like to hear a new song I'd just heard on the West Coast. He nodded his head, 'Yes,' so I sang it to him and Bea and Mom who came out of the kitchen to listen.

The Lord helped me select the right pitch, just a trifle lower than the original key in which that lovely chorus is written. I'm a "barrel-tone," you see, and can't hit high notes too gracefully. I vocalize like a drowning sailor—my scale range dies at C (sea). I've often told folks my voice sounds like the mating call of two nasal sprays. One fellow said—and I'll never forget it—"Bill, I'd like your singing if it wasn't for two things: my ears."

Anyhow, I was inspired as I sang that evening for my Dad. When I finished, tears welled in a tired pair of eyes. His reaction? "Son, sing that again. That's the sweetest chorus I think I've ever heard. It exalts my Jesus."

As I repeated it, Bea joined in with her soprano voice and Dad added his bass and we had a Weston trio. Mom sat and beamed her approval.

Dear ones, that chorus opened heaven's windows and charged the atmosphere with a Divine Presence. Dad reached for his Bible and as he began to read, our wonderful Lord lifted this precious nugget of truth from His Word and let it catch fire in my father's heart. Reading from Zechariah, chapter 3, these words from verse two came to life: "And the LORD said unto Satan, The LORD rebuke thee, O Satan; even the LORD that hath chosen Jerusalem rebuke thee: is not this a brand plucked out of the fire?"

As he read those last ten words, Dad's eyes came alive. His face became radiant, aglow, as though a bright floodlight had suddenly been turned on. Then, a shout came from his lips. "Praise God! I'm that branch!" he exclaimed. His hands were reaching toward heaven and now, a torrent of praises were issuing forth from his mouth, all glory to the Most High God.

Our Dad, our loved one, came out of the deep depression that had harnessed his mind, that had engulfed him those long desolate weeks from the last of April into these last hours of the month of June.

What happened next, we'll never forget. The eternal, loving God had paid us a visit. He was in the room. Truly heaven came down to our souls and glory crowned the Mercy Seat. The gloom of Satan's hellish oppression was gone. Bea, along with Dad, was shouting praises to the Lord. Mom was weeping joyously. And, yours truly, well, I was (of all things) laughing almost hysterically. Our dear Lord in heaven knows I had never laughed like that before. It was such a different laughter.

My Aunt Molly, a dear saint of God, used to laugh like that when she'd get blessed. As a kid, I'd look at her, wondering what in the world's gotten into Aunt Molly? I'd be grinning, of course, because her joy in the Lord, as she called it, was contagious. Everybody around her would be smiling or laughing along with her. The only thing I can figure is that since she was such close kinfolk (Dad's sister), I guess I was in line to inherit something from Aunt Molly. Anyway, here I was doing the same thing she used to do, and I couldn't stop, no-how. It was soooo great! I felt so absolutely wonderful. Oh, my! What a blessed, precious, unforgettable experience! But best of all, Dad was out from under the cloud that had shrouded his room in gloom for all those weary weeks. Victory was ours, praise the Lord!

In his Bible that I now use in my ministry, you'll find this verse underscored: Zechariah 3:2. And in the margin, next to it, in Dad's handwriting—"June 28, 1964—Hallelujah!" Yes, the hand of the oppressor had been lifted and though Dad continued to deteriorate physically, Satan's designs to further plague Dad's mind, his evil devices to thwart a victorious homegoing, were thoroughly and permanently throttled and dealt with. Amen!

I flew back to St. Louis to cover our Youth For Christ rally programs in July. Before leaving, Dad said to me, "I'm not sure I'll be able to handle any more of my meeting commitments, Son. Do you think you might possibly be able to arrange your own busy schedule and help me with a few of those meetings? I'm thinking of one in particular, the camp meeting at Springtown, Pennsylvania. You were to be with me there anyway as youth speaker and to take care of the musical program. Would you feel free, Son, to perhaps take my place as the evangelist? I'd contact them and arrange it, if you would."

My heart dropped into my boots. "What are you trying to say, Dad? Fill your shoes? How could I possibly do that?" To myself I said, *Dad, I can't.* Then it hit me. The roof caved in. My thoughts swirled. I suddenly realized my dad was not planning to hold any more meetings.

Though I didn't want to accept it, inside I knew his ministry was terminated. He was trying to break that news to me as tactfully as he could. A cold chill swept through my frame. *Dad's not going to recover. This will be his last illness. He's going home. No, I won't accept this. What will I do? This can't be. Things have just got to get back to normal here: Dad in meetings again; me joining him from time to time, as I can get free from YFC commitments. This has to go on and on and on.* Sure, I knew he was eighty-two, that he was so very tired, so very ill, but yet none of us had ever given one thought that he couldn't go on forever. Die? Not Dad.

All of this raced through my mind as I sought an answer to his question about Springtown Camp. This was the last of June. Surely by the end of August, two months away, he'd be up and about again and able to preach himself at that camp meeting. So I finally replied, "Look, Dad, that's two months away. Let's just wait and see how you're doing by then, and then we'll formulate any future plans." He smiled and said, "All right, Son." As I look back now I really feel he knew his earthly sojourn would soon be over. He'd fought a good fight, had surely kept the faith, and now, weary with the conflict, he was rather anticipating that last trip. No, not by plane or train or car down here, but through that valley referred to in Psalm 23. He wouldn't need his big old suitcase. He was going to shed these old earthly garments, put on a new robe provided by his heavenly Father, and, with the Good Shepherd leading the way, walk through wide open gates into that city, Four Square.

It was truly a hard and tearful parting for me on that occasion. As I headed for the Pittsburgh Airport and a flight back to St. Louis, I had a premonition, a sort of grim foreboding, a feeling gnawing deep down in my innards that I wouldn't see Dad again in this world.

I kept in touch by phone and Mom, Bea or Bob would report on Dad's daily progress or lack of same. I won't soon forget a call from Bea on Saturday, August 15, 1964. She was weeping. Dad had just hemorrhaged. The end was very near. Dr. Howder, a true family friend and a man who really loved his friend, Will, had come at their request to see if he couldn't perhaps give Dad a sedative to alleviate the now severe pain.

As I said previously, from the time he'd been so divinely delivered in Miami, Florida at age forty-four, my father couldn't take drugs of any kind. He reacted violently to them and Dr. Howder knew this. He mentioned this now to Dad and his weak voice replied, "I think maybe my Lord will permit it this time, Doc."

With this approval, the doctor proceeded to give him just one quarter of the average dosage. The reaction to the hypo was almost immediate. My loved ones present heard Dad whisper, "Oh, thank you, Lord! Thank you, Lord! Oh, what blessed relief! For the first time in nearly two years, no pain." Suddenly, our family realized it wasn't just the tremendous loss of blood through a serious hand injury, not just some virus or minor ailment, but that something major was the reason for the rapid deterioration of that once virile body.

In replying to Bea's call I said, "Tell Dad to hold on. I'll be there on the first plane out of St. Louis to Pittsburgh."

I heard her convey that message to Dad, and I could faintly hear his voice answering. There were some more moments of waiting and then Bea asked, "Bill, don't you have to speak at some meeting tomorrow [Sunday night]? Dad seems to recall that from your schedule you sent to us."

I answered, "Yes, I'm supposed to be at a big area-wide youth rally in Fairfield, Illinois at the First Methodist Church, but I'll call them right away. They'll understand my need to head for home. This is an emergency and I want to be with Dad."

There was more conversation at the other end of the line, and then this further word: "Bill, Dad says you must not cancel. The Lord's work comes first and they're expecting you to be there. He wants you to go. He says the Lord will take care of things at this end, that we'll be praying for you and the success of your ministry with those young people. Then, if you can, plan to fly in on Monday and I'll meet you at the airport."

My answering argument was futile.

His reply, via Bea: "Please, Son, do this for Dad. I'll be praying for you, boy, for a real outpouring of God on that youth meeting. Thanks, Son. I love you."

Those were his last words, his last message to me.

How many times, when away from home and loved ones and lonely feelings would engulf me, I would get so homesick that I thought I couldn't go on in this evangelistic ministry any longer. In those dark moments I have often relived, reechoed those last words of Dad: "The Lord's work comes first, and please, Son, do this for Dad. Thanks, Son. I love you." Then I'd read again the Master's words in Matthew 19:29: "And every one that hath forsaken houses, or brethren, or sisters, or father, or mother, or wife, or children, or lands, for my name's sake, shall receive an hundredfold, and shall inherit everlasting life." And then my heart would respond with a quiet "Amen!"

With heart aching, eyes swimming with tears, I thought, *Okay, Dad. If that's the way you want it, I'll go and then come home on the first plane Monday.*

The Sunday morning trip to that southern Illinois town was so very long. Every mile of the way I was thinking, *Bill, you should've gone home. These folks would understand. They'd have released you from this engagement.* Finally, I arrived at the church in Fairfield. It was a splendid youth conclave. The auditorium was packed with teenagers. Someone said at least 500 young people were on hand. But I don't know what I said that evening, my heart was so heavy. One I loved so very dearly was barely hanging on and I felt I should be there with him.

The Lord did bless, however—and oh, so wonderfully! Scores of youngsters responded to an altar of prayer. The Holy Spirit was at work in a very marked manner. A big football player was among those who accepted Christ that evening. He was a ponderous fellow, about six-feet-five and 250 pounds. I was told later he'd made a tackle position on the small-college All-American team. This I know, his salvation experience was very real to him.

There was a visiting time with dear friends following the meeting, then about 10:30 p.m. I headed back for the hub city of America (St. Louis). Again the miles seemed to drag on interminably. I thought I'd never get home. I finally arrived there about one o'clock in the morning. Dog tired, I crawled into bed.

Restful sleep wasn't to be my portion that night, however. About five a.m., the telephone rang. My wife, Sally, quickly answered, then handed the phone to me. It was Bea. The message through her tears was simple: "Daddy's slipped into a coma, Bill, and I think he's dying."

My reply, I'm afraid, was a wee bit tinged with bitterness. I felt I'd been denied some extra living moments with my Dad that I might've had if they hadn't been so insistent that I go to that meeting in southern Illinois. "See now, Sis, if I'd come home when I wanted to I'd have been there now."

My heart seemed to be broken. Sure, I was upset. That kind of news will upset anybody. And then I quickly repented, asking forgiveness for any sharpness in my voice, for I remembered I'd done what Dad had asked me to do. His last request of me I'd obeyed, and Bea understood. She always did. What a precious sister she's been through the years.

Hanging up the receiver, I called the airport and got a reservation on the first plane. It was an emergency and those ticket agents were so very cooperative in arranging everything for me to be aboard the first flight to Pittsburgh. I hurriedly dressed, packed a few things, had lifted the garage door and was about to get into my car when I heard the phone ring again.

It had to be my sister and I knew, I knew before I lifted the receiver, what the message would be. "Bill, Daddy's gone. He's home. No more suffering." We wept together over those miles of wires. A few more words of conversation and the receiver was put back on the hook.

There was no need to hurry now so I canceled the plane reservation. It's funny how thoughts like that seem so important or can be recalled so vividly. My wife, Sally, hugged me close and quietly said through her tears, "I'll get ready, honey, and we can drive back home together now."

There was a light drizzle of rain as we started that long homeward trek. The action of the windshield wipers made me think of that verse, "God shall wipe away all tears from their eyes" (Revelation 21:4) and I thought, *I guess even heaven is joining us in our grief this morning.* Those 600-plus miles of highway found us reliving past memories, times spent with our loved one through those unforgettable years.

Arriving in that little town of Elizabeth, Pennsylvania, we went immediately to the funeral home.

The undertaker met us at the door. He informed us that Mother and Bea had just returned a few moments before to the old homestead on Center Avenue. As we walked on into the parlor, there by Dad's casket, keeping a lonely vigil, was my precious brother, Bob. I put my hand on his shoulder.

Turning and seeing it was me, he buried his head on my neck and let all the aches of a thoroughly crushed heart spill out through tears. His first words were, "Bill, who's going to pray for us now?"

Bless his dear heart, I was so glad for these words that came to mind—inspired of the Master I'm sure—to comfort my brother. "Bob, I don't think Dad has forgotten us," I said. "He was so tired, had such a long and blessed ministry. He's home now; and ya know, pal, if God hadn't been so good to us as a family by raising Dad up, back there when he'd been sent away to die, well, really you'd have never remembered Dad because you were just a babe in arms then. God was so good in allowing us to have Dad an added thirty-eight years."

My brother looked at me for a long moment. As he wiped tears away, he said, "I hadn't thought of that, Bill. Yes, God was so good to allow me those years with Dad."

Fresh tears flowed as we two brothers, who dearly loved that one lying there before us, found consolation in this fact: Our great heavenly Father doeth all things well (Mark 7:37).

I can't prove this—it's the way my mind operates and you can't prove it couldn't be so—but I think many of his friends were there at the gate to greet him as he entered: "Hello, Will. Welcome home." I'm certain his mother's greeting was something like this: "Hello, Billy." Then with a knowing smile, she probably said, "I told you you'd preach. Remember, Son?" And, of course, the Savior would be there: "Well done, Son! Welcome home."

As I travel now, how thrilled I am to meet folks everywhere I go who come up to me and say marvelous things about Dad and his ministry.

"Bill, I was saved through your dad's ministry. My husband, too."

"My daughter was healed when Brother Weston prayed for her."

"Our baby was delivered when Daddy Weston prayed. We'll never forget him."

"I dedicated my life to the ministry—I'm a missionary, I'm a pastor, etc., etc.,—through your dad's ministry."

Literally hundreds of times I have heard words like these. And then there have been so many who've been kind in saying, "Bill, you look more and more like your dad." What a super-special compliment that is! Or those who've really thrilled me—and truly humbled me—by saying, "Your dad's mantle has fallen on you." And, I'd think, *Dear Lord, how I wish, how I long that this could be so.*

But you see, I soon get back to reality. I'm a nut, and always have been. It sort of makes a fellow wonder how he, being as he is, could've been birthed by the likes of Tessie and Will Weston. One dear old soul told me one time, "Bill, you're the craziest thing." She didn't elaborate, didn't smile, just said that and passed on through the doorway, where I was greeting people. I didn't rightly know just how she meant that. *Crazy peculiar or funny-ha-ha?* I found solace a little later from the

Psalm that says, "The LORD preserveth the simple" (Psalm 116:6).

In a meeting in Hialeah, Florida recently, a man truly blessed me with this memory of Dad. He said, "Bill, the first time I ever saw your dad was at Delta Lake Camp Meeting near Rome, New York. I didn't know him, never had met him or heard him preach until that time. I was sitting in the tabernacle there one evening listening to the preliminaries, music, etc., when all of a sudden, I sensed a presence in that big auditorium. Rather startled, I looked up, turned my head to see what caused this strange feeling and this man—your father—was walking toward the platform. Bill, I repeat this, I didn't know your dad, but before God I say this: before seeing him I had felt his presence and I thought to myself, he's a man of God. And Bill, I'm sure, the thousand or more people there must've felt the same thing that I did. I'll never forget that moment and I just had to come up here and share that experience with you."

I treasure that testimony. I couldn't have heard anything more complimentary than those words about a dad that I, and all our family, knew lived in unbroken fellowship with his Master and Lord. Even now, when we are ill, facing problems, or needing answers, we still feel that if only Dad could be present everything would be all right. When he prayed we expected answers.

Now, as I see it, he and Mother have been reunited. They are together again, and knowing them so well, I figure they're awaiting the arrival of the rest of the Weston clan. They've bottled up prayers on our behalf, and I'm sure they're trusting for an unbroken family circle to be present for the greatest of all occasions, the Marriage Supper of the Lamb. Yes, bless the Lord, He is truly worthy, the Lamb that was slain.

My! I can't believe a fellow who hates to write as much as I do, could have possibly scrawled so long an epistle. Anyhow, after reading this, and I trust you will, I can't help but feel you'll maybe smile and in agreement say, "My, wotta dad Bill had!"